Charles Edwin Prescott

New York; its past and present, compiled for the exclusive use of the traveling public

Charles Edwin Prescott

New York; its past and present, compiled for the exclusive use of the traveling public

ISBN/EAN: 9783337208493

Printed in Europe, USA, Canada, Australia, Japan

Cover: Foto ©Andreas Hilbeck / pixelio.de

More available books at **www.hansebooks.com**

ITS

PAST AND PRESENT.

COMPILED FOR THE EXCLUSIVE USE

OF

THE TRAVELING PUBLIC.

BY

C. H. PRESCOTT.

NEW YORK:
Published by the Mercantile Publishing Co.,
NO. 1 PARK PLACE.
1874.

Entered according to Act of Congress, in the year 1874, by
THE MERCANTILE PUBLISHING COMPANY, in the Office of
the Librarian of Congress, at Washington.

Electrotyped and Printed by
McDonald, Dillont & Co.,
No. 1 Park Place, cor. Broadway, N. Y.

PREFACE.

The stranger who visits the city of New York for the first time, naturally desires to know something more about the "Metropolis of the New World" than have been afforded him by the meagre accounts that he has from time to time seen. There are many interesting localities, scattered in and around the city, and its suburbs, that are unknown, even to residents of many years; the endeavor in this work has been to collect them under appropriate headings, and to give such brief descriptions as may serve more fully to guide the stranger to their whereabouts. The entire edition has been placed in the suites of rooms of the following hotels:

BREVOORT,	EVERETT,	GRAND CENTRAL,	ST. JAMES,
CLARENDON,	FIFTH AVENUE,	HOFFMAN,	ST. NICHOLAS,
COLEMAN,	GILSEY,	METROPOLITAN,	STURTEVANT,
EARLE'S,	GRAND,	NEW YORK,	WINDSOR.

Copies may also be procured at the office of publication,

NO. 1 PARK PLACE.

Particular attention is called to the advertisements: they are those of strictly first-class establishments that invite the reader's patronage.

NEW YORK, Nov. 1st, 1874.

SYNOPSIS OF CONTENTS.

NEW YORK CITY.

INTRODUCTION—HISTORICAL SKETCH—HISTORICAL LOCALITIES,   Page. 7–45

CENTRAL PARK.

ORIGIN AND EARLY HISTORY—LOCATION AND AREA—CARRIAGE SERVICE—PARK KEEPERS—GATEWAYS AND APPROACHES—NAMES OF GATES—THOROUGHFARES—RESERVOIRS—GENERAL FEATURES—LOWER PARK—HUMBOLDT MONUMENT—STATUE OF COMMERCE—THE POND—MUSEUM—THE DAIRY—THE KINDER-BERG—BALL GROUND—CAROUSAL—SEVENTH REGIMENT MEMORIAL—THE MARBLE ARCH—INDIAN HUNTER—THE GREEN—THE SPA—THE MALL—MUSIC STAND—PERGOLA—CARRIAGE CONCOURSE—THE CASINO—MORSE STATUE—"AULD LANG SYNE"—"THE TIGRESS"—TERRACE—BETHESDA FOUNTAIN—THE LAKE—RAMBLE—MONUMENT TO SCHILLER—THE CAVE—BELVIDERE—TUNNEL—CONSERVATORY WATER—DEER PARK—METROPOLITAN MUSEUM OF ART—THE MAZE—MUSEUM OF NATURAL HISTORY—THE KNOLL—THE UPPER PARK—MOUNT ST. VINCENT—FORTIFICATIONS—BLOCK HOUSE—POOL, LOCH, AND HARLEM MEER—THE GREAT HILL—HOW TO GO TO THE PARK, ... 47–91

PARKS AND PUBLIC SQUARES.

THE BATTERY—BOWLING GREEN—CITY HALL PARK—WASHINGTON SQUARE—UNION SQUARE—GRAMMERCY PARK—STUYVESANT PARK—TOMPKINS SQUARE—MADISON SQUARE—RESERVOIR PARK—MT. MORRIS SQUARE—RIVERSIDE PARK—MORNINGSIDE PARK, ... 93–99

THEATRES.

ACADEMY OF MUSIC—BOOTH'S—BRYANT'S—COLOSSEUM—NIBLO'S—OLYMPIC—PARK—UNION SQUARE—WALLACK'S, . 101–115

PUBLIC BUILDINGS.

CITY HALL—NEW COURT HOUSE—HALL OF RECORDS—HALLS OF JUSTICE—DEPARTMENT OF CHARITIES AND CORRECTION—CITY ARMORIES—CUSTOM HOUSE—UNITED STATES TREASURY AND ASSAY OFFICE—OLD POST OFFICE—NEW POST OFFICE—GRAND CENTRAL RAILWAY STATION—MARKETS, ... 117–124

PUBLIC WORKS.

CROTON AQUEDUCT—HIGH BRIDGE—EAST RIVER BRIDGE—HARLEM BRIDGE, ... 125–128

CONTENTS.   v

BENEVOLENT INSTITUTIONS.

BLACKWELL'S ISLAND—RANDALL'S ISLAND—BLOOMINGDALE ASYLUM FOR THE INSANE—NEW YORK JUVENILE ASYLUM—NEW YORK ORPHAN ASYLUM—MAGDALENE ASYLUM—ASYLUM FOR AGED INDIGENT FEMALES—INSTITUTION FOR THE BLIND—INSTITUTION FOR THE DEAF AND DUMB—HOUSE OF INDUSTRY—HOME FOR THE FRIENDLESS—LEAKE AND WATTS ORPHAN HOUSE—SOCIETY FOR THE RELIEF OF WIDOWS AND SMALL CHILDREN—NEW YORK DISPENSARIES—DEMILT DISPENSARY—BELLEVUE HOSPITAL—ST. LUKE'S HOSPITAL SAILORS' SNUG HARBOR, ... 129–135

SOCIETIES AND ASSOCIATIONS.

YOUNG MEN'S CHRISTIAN ASSOCIATION—COOPER UNION—I. O. OF O. F.—AMERICAN ETHNOLOGICAL SOCIETY—AMERICAN BIBLE SOCIETY—NEW YORK HISTORICAL SOCIETY—NATIONAL ACADEMY OF DESIGN—LYCEUM OF NATURAL HISTORY—METROPOLITAN MUSEUM OF ART—NATIONAL RIFLE ASSOCIATION, ... 136–143

LIBRARIES.

ASTOR LIBRARY—SOCIETY LIBRARY—MERCANTILE LIBRARY—APPRENTICES' LIBRARY, ... 144–146

COLLEGES AND SEMINARIES.

COLLEGE OF THE CITY OF NEW YORK—NEW YORK UNIVERSITY—COLUMBIA COLLEGE—COLLEGE OF ST. FRANCIS XAVIER—MANHATTAN COLLEGE—UNION THEOLOGICAL SEMINARY—COLLEGE OF PHYSICIANS AND SURGEONS—NEW YORK MEDICAL COLLEGE—UNIVERSITY MEDICAL COLLEGE—N. Y. MEDICAL COLLEGE AND HOSPITAL FOR WOMEN, ... 146–149

CHURCHES.

TRINITY—GRACE—ST. GEORGE'S—ST. PAUL'S—ST. JOHN'S—ST. MARK'S TRANSFIGURATION—ST. PATRICK'S CATHEDRAL—CHURCH OF THE MESSIAH—CHURCH OF ALL SOULS—DUTCH REFORMED—FOURTH UNIVERSALIST—ST. PAUL'S METHODIST EPISCOPAL—FIRST BAPTIST—BRICK CHURCH, ... 150–158

CEMETERY.

GREENWOOD, ... 158–163

SUBURBS.

BROOKLYN—NAVY YARD—STATEN ISLAND—HOBOKEN—FLUSHING—GOVERNOR'S ISLAND—FORT HAMILTON—CONEY ISLAND—LONG BRANCH—ROCKAWAY—JAMAICA—THROG'S POINT—ASTORIA—MONTAUK—CROTON DAM—CREEDMOOR, ... 163–169

FORTIFICATIONS.

FORT TOMKINS—FORT RICHMOND—FORT LAFAYETTE—FORT HAMILTON FORT COLUMBUS—CASTLE WILLIAM—FORT SCHUYLER, . . . 169–170

DIRECTORY TO ADVERTISEMENTS.

THE GORHAM CO.
SILVERSMITHS.

[ESTABLISHED 1831.]

Salesrooms, No. 1 Bond Street, New York.

Leading Silversmiths. The Gorham Company constantly employ a larger number of workmen on Solid Silver Ware than any other manufacturers in the world.

Purest Silver. Every ounce of Silver made by them bears their Stamp or Trade Mark, thus: and is absolutely guaranteed sterling purity, 925–1,000 fine. **STERLING**

Original Designs. They have earned a wide reputation for the select character, great beauty and excellence of their designs. Attention is called to a variety of an antique type just completed.

Largest Stock. The richest and largest assortment of choice articles for Wedding and Testimonial Gifts and general family use, to be found in the country.

Bridal Gifts. A great variety, all that are necessary in common table use, as well as the most elaborate and complete wedding outfit.

THE GORHAM COMPANY

are also the exclusive manufacturers of the celebrated Gorham

ELECTRO-PLATE

Tea Sets, Dinner Services, &c., &c.

THE BEST PLATED WARE IN THE WORLD.

AT RETAIL,

At Salesrooms of the Company,

No. 1 Bond Street, near Broadway, New York.

NEW YORK;

ITS PAST AND PRESENT.

The City of New York, from its geographical position, having become the great centre of commercial enterprise, is justly regarded as the Metropolitan City of the New World. In mercantile importance it bears the same relation to the United States that London does to Great Britain. Its past history is replete with interest, for it has been the theatre of some of the most important events that pertain to our country's memorable career; and although it possesses fewer historic shrines than are to be found in many cities of the Old World, yet its chronicles still live as treasured relics in the hearts of its people, and on the pages of its national records. If we take a retrospective glance we shall find that a little more than two centuries ago, this island of *Mannahata*—its earliest recorded name—had its birth-day of civilization in a few rude huts, and a fort situated where the Bowling Green now stands; and in this comparatively brief interval in the lifetime of a nation, it has bounded from the infant *Dorp* or village, into a noble city of palaces, with its million of inhabitants. It is now the greatest workshop of the Western World—the busy hive of industry, with its tens of thousands of artisans, mechanics and merchants, sending out, to all sections of its wide-spread domain, the magic

CULBERT & CO.,

No. 24 Maiden Lane,

Importers of

LONDON, PARIS AND VIENNA LEATHER GOODS,

TRAVELING BAGS

(Furnished and Unfurnished),

In Russia Leather, Canvas and Morocco.

TOURISTS' BAGS, LADIES' SHOPPING BAGS,

Russia Leather and Morocco,

Jewel Boxes, Dressing Cases, Work Boxes, Glove and Handkerchief Boxes, Segar Cases, Match Boxes, Card Cases, Pocket Books, Portfolios, Writing Cases and Desks, Ladies' Companions, Shawl Straps, Collar Boxes, etc.

FINE WRITING DESKS,

In ROSEWOOD, AMBOINE, BLACK WALNUT, ASH, and other fancy woods.

These Desks are all made with our Patent Flap, expressly for our Retail Trade.

ALL GOODS MARKED IN PLAIN FIGURES.

Fine Electro Silver-Plated Goods,

— FOR —

Wedding & Holiday Gifts

AND

GENERAL FAMILY USE.

These Wares are absolutely and unequivocally

GUARANTEED

To be of the

FINEST GRADE

And are offered at the

Most Reasonable Rates.

B. LANDER,

18 John Street, New York.

(Old Ware Repaired and Replated equal to new.)

of machinery for all departments of handicraft, and argosies of magnificent vessels for garnering in the wealth of foreign climes.

If we glance prospectively, how shall we venture to limit its progressive march in opulence and greatness? In less than half a century hence, it will doubtless double its present numerical importance. As illustrations of the enormous increase in the value of real estate, it may be mentioned that a lot, on the north-west corner of Chambers street and Broadway, was purchased by a gentleman who died in 1858, for $1,000. Its present value is now estimated at no less a sum than $150,000.

The site on which the new *Herald* Building now stands was purchased by James Gordon Bennett, Esq., for $400,000 paid to Barnum for an unexpired lease of thirteen years, held at the time his American Museum was burned. Also, the lot immediately adjoining this, with a frontage of less than sixty feet on Broadway, was sold at auction for $310,000!

A little more than two centuries since, the entire site of this noble city was purchased of the Indians for what was equivalent to the nominal sum of $24. Now the assessed value of its real estate exceeds $550,000,000. If such vast accessions of wealth have characterized the history of the past, who shall compute the constantly augmenting resources of its onward course? Half a century ago the uses of the mighty agents of steam and the electric current were unknown; now the whole surface of our vast country is threaded over with a network of railroads, and our seas, lakes and rivers, are thickly studded with steamers; stately vessels freighted with the fruits of commerce, all tending to this city as the central mart of trade. Half a century ago it took weeks to transmit news from New York to New Orleans, now our communications are conveyed over the length and breadth of the land almost with the velocity of the lightning's flash. Within a

Ladies', Gents and Children's

SHOES.

Largest Assortment of the Best Quality in the City.

1141 BROADWAY,

Cor. 26th Street,

—AND—

858 BROADWAY,

Bet. 13th & 14th Sts.

like interval the most rapid printing-press was slowly worked by hand-power. Now the winged messengers of intelligence are multiplied with the marvelous rapidity of 60,000 copies an hour. While the mechanic arts have thus revolutionized the social condition of the past, a corresponding change has marked its history in the establishment of numerous schools of learning, diffusing their beneficent influence on the minds and morals of the masses.

Then, again, as respects its costly stores and private residences, New York seems to vie with London and Paris. All along Broadway and its intersecting streets, the eye is greeted everywhere by long lines of marble and stone buildings, many of them of great architectural elegance. The several broad avenues and squares in the upper part of the city are studded with a succession of splendid mansions, in some instances costing from $50,000 to $200,000 each. There are, it is estimated, some three hundred churches, many of them of costly and magnificent proportions; while its superb hotels—the boast of the metropolis—are, in some instances, capable of accommodating about one thousand guests.

How mighty and far-reaching must its influences become in its future progress it were difficult to compute, since its numerical extent, numbering at present, if we include Brooklyn and the adjacent places on the west, over a millon and a half of souls, will ere long place it in the scale of cities of the world, in the foremost rank.

Society in New York has many phases, it is cosmopolitan and amalgam, composed of all imaginable varieties and shades of character. It is a confluence of many streams, whose waters are ever turbid and confused in their rushing to this great vortex. What incongruous elements are here commingled: the rude and the refined, the sordid and the self-sacrificing, the religious and the profane, the learned and the illiterate, the affluent and the destitute, the thinker

230 FIFTH AVENUE,

Bet. 26th & 27th Sts.,   NEW YORK.

Rich Paris Embroideries, Berlin Zephyr Worsteds,

Filet Guipure,

AND ALL ARTICLES NEEDED FOR WORSTED WORK.

Babies' Sacks, Hoods and Afghans of the finest quality ONLY.

Mouchoir Cases, Jewelry Boxes, and Russia Leather Goods,

HANDSOME BASKETS, BAMBOO WORK STANDS, SLIPPER CASES,

TOWEL AND HAT RACKS, SCREENS, Etc.,

EMBROIDERING, STAMPING AND DESIGNING.

FINE FURS.

THE BEST AND FINEST FURS IN THE CITY.

Shetland Seal Sacks a Specialty,

In which we especially can offer a great inducement.

CHINCHILLA, SILVER FOX, ERMINE, ETC., ETC.

Large and select line for children.

Fur Trimmings in Great Variety,

GENTS' SEAL COATS, CAPS, ROBES, ETC.

M. MAHLER,

Importer and Manufacturer,

849 BROADWAY, { Between Thirteenth and Fourteenth Streets. } NEW YORK.

and the doer, the virtuous and the ignoble, the young and the aged, all nations, dialects, and sympathies, all habits, manners and customs of the civilized globe.

City life everywhere presents protean aspects. Let us take a glance at some of its most striking features, notwithstanding the mixed multitudes that are incessantly thronging its various avenues. There are yet certain localities that exhibit distinct characteristics; life in Wall street presents an epitomized view of its mercantile phase. Here are its banks, its money exchanges, and their great place of rendezvous, the Exchange, beneath the dome of which many mighty projects have had their birth. Here have been concocted vast schemes of commercial enterprise, and here, too, have originated many noble acts of public benefaction.

Up Nassau street, to its junction with Chatham street, of mock auction notoriety, we catch a glimpse of another phase of city life. To denizens of New York, society is usually known under the generic divisions of *Broadway* and *Bowery*. Each has its distinct idiosyncrasies; the former being regarded as patrician, and the latter as plebeian. Looking at New York longitudinally, we may say that Fourteenth street, at present, marks the boundary of the great workshop. In the precincts of Madison Square and the Fifth avenue, we find monuments of the wealth, taste and splendor of its citizens.

The southern part of the city—its original site—exhibits all kinds of irregularity; the streets are narrow, sinuous and uneven in their surface; but the northern or upper portion is laid out at right angles. There are some twelve fine avenues, at parallel distances apart of about 800 feet. There are about 300 miles of paved streets in the Metropolis, extending to Fifty-ninth street; exclusive of projected streets not yet paved, over 100 streets more. The city has been laid out and surveyed to the extent of 12 miles from the Battery.

LOVE'S,

313 6th Avenue, bet. 19th & 20th Sts.,

Manufacturer of

HAND-MADE WORSTED GOODS

FOR LADIES AND CHILDREN.

Hoods, Caps, Sacks, Cloaks, Shirts, Drawers, Leggins, Bootees, Mitts, Scarfs, Veils, Shawls, Etc., Afghans from $5 up,

WHOLESALE AND RETAIL.

Our PATENT SILK CAP, delicate, soft, light and beautiful, recommended by Physicians.

☞ BRANCH STORE, 1197 BROADWAY, Between 28th and 29th STREETS.

| SPECIALTY. |

ENGLISH CASSIMERE TROUSERS,

$10 to Order.

WILLMONT,

663 Broadway, N. Y.

N. B.—FINE CUSTOM CLOTHING TO ORDER.

Perhaps the most dense part of the Metropolis—its very heart, from whence issues the vitalizing tide of its commerce—is the junction of Broadway and Fulton street, and its vicinity. The collision of interests which all the stir and traffic of those crowded streets involve brings human nature into strong relief, and intensifies the lights and shades of character.

It is in these dusty avenues to wealth, these vestibules where fraud contends with honor for an entrance into the temple, that we read the heart of man better than in books.

The great characteristic of New York is din and excitement, everything to be done in a hurry, all is intense anxiety. It is especially noticeable in the great thoroughfare of Broadway, where the noise and confusion caused by the incessant passing and repassing of some 20,000 vehicles a day render it a Babel scene of confusion.

New York has ever been, and justly, renowned for its Catholic and liberal public benefactions and charities. Among her many glories this is most conspicuous. New York may be called the asylum for the oppressed and distressed of all nations. Abounding in beneficent institutions suited to the relief of the various "ills that flesh is heir to," and enriched with the most liberal endowments for classical and popular instruction, she bears the palm in all that pertains to the moral, intellectual and physical advancement of society. It is true we are a mercantile and money-making people, but the empire city is an illustration of some of its noblest uses.

By way of introduction to the city in detail, we recommend the visitor first to get a bird's-eye view of it from the steeple of Trinity Church. A view from this elevation—over 280 feet in height—affords a good idea of the general extent and topography of the city. The tower is accessible to the public at any time of the day, excepting the hours devoted to divine service, morning and afternoon. To facilitate the

JAMES L. FLING,
178 Fifth Avenue,

GENTS' FURNISHING GOODS,
Underwear and Hosiery
IN ALL THE FINE GRADES.

Ladies' and Gents' Alexandrine Kid Gloves,
The Only Agency of these Goods in this Country.

FINE CUSTOM SHIRTS A SPECIALTY.
London and Paris Novelties.

IMPERIAL
Russian Vapor Baths,
Unequaled in Elegance, Luxury and Sanitary Value.
MARBLE SHOWER, VAPOR & PLUNGE ROOMS.
Private Departments for all who prefer.

SPECIAL LADIES' DEPARTMENT.

These Baths are a most agreeable luxury. They promote health by cleansing the pores of all impurities and rendering the skin active and vigorous. They relieve colds, rheumatism, neuralgia, nervousness, sleeplessness, etc. To ladies they offer the best and safest cosmetic, clearing the complexion and leaving no taint behind. Call and inspect, whether you bathe or not.

— ALSO —

SULPHUR & OTHER MEDICINAL BATH DEPARTMENTS.
No. 7 W. 24th Street,
(OPPOSITE FIFTH AVENUE HOTEL.)

ascent of the church tower there are landing places. At the first of these you have a fine view of the interior of this cathedral-like edifice; at the next resting place is the belfry, with its solemn chimes. Here, too, is a balcony, allowing us a first view of the city. Still higher up we gain a magnificent panoramic view of all we have left below us, which amply repays our toilsome tour of many steps. The variegated scene stretches out in every direction, with new beauties—north and south lies Broadway, with its teeming multitudes and numberless vehicles; west and east are crowded streets of house-tops, terminating only with the waters of the enclosing rivers. Looking eastward, we see Wall street immediately below us, with the Treasury Building on the left, and a little further on the right the Custom House, the Wall Street Ferry, and the East River, which separates New York from Brooklyn, with the New York Bay stretching to the south-east, Sandy Hook, the Highlands of Neversink and the coast of Staten Island. To the north-east, the eastern district of Brooklyn, formerly known as Williamsburgh, the Navy Yard, etc., and still further to the north, the rocky channel called *Helle-Gaat*, so perilous to our Dutch forefathers; near by Randall and Blackwell's Islands, with their City Asylums. Transferring our gaze to Broadway, we notice the Equitable Life Insurance Building, and Mutual Life Insurance Co.'s Building, which stand higher than all others, and on the next block the Western Union Telegraph Building just completed. Further on we notice the *Herald* and Park Bank Buildings, corner of Ann street, on the east side of Broadway, and opposite to them, St. Paul's Church, then the Astor House, the New Post Office in the Park, and the City Hall; the brown stone building on the east side being that of the *Times* Office, opposite to which the Tribune Association are now erecting a magnificent building which shall serve at once as an office for their paper, and as a lasting monument to the genius of

KNICKERBOCKER
Life Insurance Company,

239 BROADWAY, N. Y.

JOHN A. NICHOLS, - - President.

Accumulated Assets, Jan. 1, 1874, - - $8,087,211.02
Gross Liabilities, including reserve, - 6,909,968.29
Surplus as to Policy-Holders, - - - 1,177,243.73

Ratio of Expenses (including taxes) to Total Income, 13-47.

A RETURN PREMIUM (dividend) will be apportioned to each Policy from the above surplus, IN PROPORTION TO ITS CONTRIBUTION thereto, available on settlement of next ANNUAL premium.

The "SAVINGS BANK PLAN," recently introduced by this Company, has proved a great success, from the fact that policies bear on their face a DEFINITE CASH SURRENDER VALUE, and are as negotiable as a Government Bond.

GEO. F. SNIFFEN, Secretary.   CHAS. M. HIBBARD, Actuary.
HENRY W. JOHNSON, Counsel.   E. W. DERBY, M. D., Consulting Phys'n.

JOHN C. DEVIN,
Importer of French Fancy Goods,

SKIRTS, CORSETS, FANS, BUSTLES, PARIS LINGERIE, SMALL WARES,

1192 Broadway, (East side,)

Under the Sturtevant House.

Attention is called to my specialty,

"THE PANSY CORSET,"

which for quality and superiority of FIT is unsurpassed.

I am in constant receipt of the celebrated three-button

GANT SWEDE,

of Jouvin's best make.

Horace Greeley. Beyond the City Hall will be noticed, in a yet unfinished condition, that Court House about which so much has been written and said. A monument to political rascality and unblushing roguery. Further north are numerous elegant stores, including Lord & Taylor's marble edifice, St. Nicholas Hotel, the Metropolitan, the Grand Central Hotel and Stewart's Marble Palace, corner of Tenth street, occupying one entire block, and the largest dry goods establishment in the world; and still further on in the distance, Grace Church, Union Square, etc.

Turning to the opposite point of view: The Hudson river, with Jersey City, and Hoboken with its beautiful walks, its distant hills and valleys; on this side are the steamers, ships and docks. This superb river has been often compared with the Rhine for its picturesque beauty. We can here get but a faint idea of it, for its bold scenery is seen only after journeying some forty miles to the north; we catch merely a glimpse of the Palisades, beginning at Weehawken and extending about twenty miles. Veering to the south, we see the fortified islets of the lower bay, with Staten Island, Richmond, etc., with their numerous picturesque cottages, villas and castellated mansions, and to the southwest, the Raritan bay, the Passaic river, leading to Newark in the distance.

HISTORICAL SKETCH.

In the year 1607, the memorable year in which forty-seven learned men began the English version of the Bible, Henry Hudson sailed in search of a north-east passage to India. For two seasons he strove in vain to penetrate the ice barriers, and then turned homeward. His patrons abandoned their enterprise, and Hudson went over to Holland and entered the

Mlle. EMILIE KUHN & CO.,

IMPORTERS OF

Zephyr Worsteds, Canvas Embroideries

AND ALL MATERIALS FOR NEEDLE WORK,

FRENCH, GERMAN AND ENGLISH FANCY GOODS, HAND-MADE WORSTED GOODS, LINEN GUIPURE, &c.

All kinds of Embroidering and Designing done to order,

LESSONS GIVEN IN ALL KINDS OF FANCY WORK,

941 BROADWAY,

Cor. 22d Street,   NEW YORK.

ALSO, AT No. 2 ATLANTIC BUILDING, LONG BRANCH.

BLANK-BOOKS, STATIONERY & PRINTING.

Francis & Loutrel,

S T A T I O N E R S

STEAM JOB PRINTERS, LITHOGRAPHERS AND MANUFACTURERS OF PATENT SPRING-BACK ACCOUNT BOOKS,

45 Maiden Lane, New York.

Orders solicited for anything in our line. Large assortment of Fancy and Staple Stationery, Account Books, Writing Paper, Hotel Registers, Time Books, Expense Books, Diaries and Daily Journals.
Copy Your Letters.—Use Francis' Manifold Writer, by which letters and copies are written at the same time. Reporters' Books, Duplicating Sheets, Carbon Paper, &c.
Merchants, Bankers, Factories, Public Offices, Railroad and Insurance Companies, as well as individuals, are solicited to give us their orders. Prompt and personal attention given. Prices low.
The entire building is fitted expressly for the various branches of our business, with new and improved Machinery, Steam Power Presses, New Type, etc. Please call or send your orders to

FRANCIS & LOUTREL,
Stationers, Printers, and Bookbinders,

LEWIS FRANCIS, }
CYRUS H. LOUTREL. }   45 MAIDEN LANE, N. Y.

Patent Composition for Printers' Inking Rollers. Does not harden, shrink, nor crack. Patent Copyable Printing Ink, all colors.

service of the Dutch East India Company, whose fleets then agitated the waters of almost every sea.

On the 3d of September, 1609, the intrepid navigator first entered the Bay of New York. Here commence the acknowledged chronicles of European civilization on these shores of the newly-discovered continent, over which, till then, the wild Indian had held undisputed sway. According to the Scandinavian records, it is affirmed, the Norsemen visited our shores even prior to the discovery of the continent by the famed Genoese.

Among those supposed early navigators was Prince Madoc; and Verrazani, who, in the year 1514, is believed to have anchored in these waters and explored the coast of what was then known as part of ancient Vinland. We shall take a cursory glance at the leading events which have been handed down to us, since they will serve to illustrate the progressive advancement of the civilized over the savage forms of life, of which this memorable island has been the theatre.

Although Hudson has not recorded in his diary his landing in the harbor of New York, we possess a tradition of the event by Heckewelder, the Indian historian. He describes the natives as greatly perplexed and terrified when they beheld the approach of the strange object—the ship in the offing. They deemed it a visit from the Manitou, coming in his big canoe, and began to prepare an entertainment for his reception. "By-and-by, the chief, *in red clothes and a glitter of metal*, with others, came ashore in a smaller canoe, mutual salutations and signs of friendship were exchanged; and after a while strong drink was offered, which made all gay and happy. In time, as their mutual acquaintance progressed, the *white skins* told them they would stay with them if they were allowed as much land for cultivation as the hide of a bullock, spread before them could cover or *encompass*. The request was granted, and the pale men

Printing.   Stationery.   Blank Books.

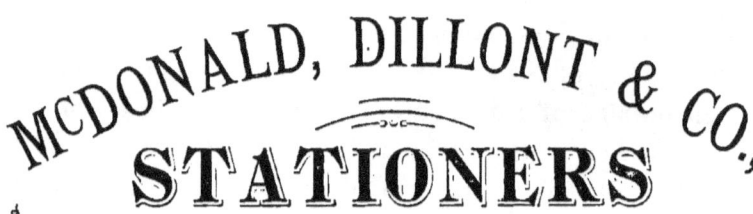

STATIONERS

LITHOGRAPHERS,

BLANK BOOK Manufacturers AND ENGRAVERS

No. 1 Park Place, Cor. Broadway,

NEW YORK.

Card Engraving.   Wedding Orders filled with despatch.   Visiting Cards and Invitations.   A large assortment of Fine, Staple and Fancy Stationery always on hand.   Baskerville Note Papers and Envelopes. Venetian Cabinets, &c., &c.   GOODALL'S PLAYING CARDS in all varieties.

ALL THE SPECIALTIES OF THE TRADE.

ORDERS FOR PRINTING OF EVERY DESCRIPTION SOLICITED.   PRICES AS LOW AS ANY OTHER RESPONSIBLE HOUSE IN THE CITY.

PLEASE CALL OR SEND YOUR ORDERS TO

McDONALD, DILLONT & CO.,

Printers and Stationers,

CORNER OF BROADWAY.   No. 1 Park Place, New York.

thereupon, beginning at a starting point on the hide, cut it up into one long extended narrow strip, or thong, sufficient to encompass a large place. Their cunning equally surprised and amused the confiding and simple Indians, who willingly allowed the success of their artifice, and backed it with a cordial welcome." Such was the origin of the site of New York, on the place called *Manhattan* (*i.e.*, Manahachtanienks) a revelling name, importing "the place where they all got drunk!" and a name *then bestowed* by the Indians as commemorative of that first great meeting.

Hudson afterward proceeded to explore the North River, since called after his name—the *Hudson*. The Half-Moon anchored at Yonkers, and the Indians came off in canoes to traffic with the strangers. But the river narrowed beyond the Highlands, and Hudson, after sailing up as far as the site of Albany, retraced his way to Manhattan, and at once sailed for Europe. His favorable reports gave rise to an expedition of two ships in 1614, under Captain Adrian Block and Hendrick Christiaanse. It was under their auspices that the first actual settlement was begun upon the site of the present New York, consisting in the first year of four houses, and in the next year of a redoubt on the site of the Bowling Green. To this small village they gave the name of New Amsterdam. The settlement was of a commercial and military character, having for its object the traffic in the fur trade.

At the time Holland projected this scheme of commercial settlement, she possessed 20,000 vessels and 100,000 mariners. The City of Amsterdam was at the head of the enterprise.

From its earliest period "Nieuw Amsterdam" had a checkered history. The English turned toward it a wistful eye, and took it from the Dutch in 1664, who succeeded, however, in recovering it in 1673. Not more than a year after it was ceded again to the British, and underwent a change of name from New Amsterdam to New York, in

TIFFANY & CO.,

UNION SQUARE, - NEW YORK.

A GREAT VARIETY OF ARTICLES SUITABLE FOR

PRIZES

FOR

YACHTING, RACING, SPORTING, ETC.,

ALL OF THEIR OWN MAKE, FROM ORIGINAL DESIGNS.

SPECIAL DESIGNS, WITH ESTIMATES, FURNISHED.

A COMPLETE ASSORTMENT OF

Stem Winders, in great variety, and new Styles of Cases.
Chronographs, marking Fifth Seconds.
Chronographs, with Split Seconds.
Chronographs, with Split and Independent Seconds.
Repeaters, striking Hours and Quarters.
Repeaters, striking Hours and Minutes.
Self-Acting Repeaters, striking Hours and Quarters.
Calendar Watches, showing Day of the Week and Month, and Changes of the Moon.

Particular Attention given to Cleaning and Repairing Fine Watches.

honor of James, Duke of York, to whom it was made over by Charles II. From this period it began to make progress, although slowly, in buildings, population, and municipal arrangements.

The city, prior to British rule (that is, in 1656), was laid out in streets, some of them crooked enough, and contained "one hundred and twenty houses with extensive garden lots," and about one thousand inhabitants. In 1677 another estimate reports that it comprised three hundred and sixty-eight houses, while its assessed property amounted to ninety-five thousand pounds sterling.

During the military rule of Governor Colve, who held the city for one year under the above mentioned capture for the States of Holland, everything partook of a military character, and the laws still in preservation at Albany show the energy of a rigorous discipline. Then the Dutch Mayor, at the head of the city militia, held his daily parades before the City Hall (Stadt Huys), then at Coenties Slip; and every evening at sunset he received from the principal guard of the fort, called the *hoofd-wagt*, the keys of the city, and thereupon proceeded, with a guard of six, to lock the city gates; then to place a *burger-wagt*, a citizen guard, as night watch, at assigned places. The same Mayor also went the rounds at sunrise to open the gates, and to restore the keys to the officers of the fort.

In 1683 the first constitutional assembly, consisting of a council of ten, and eighteen representatives, was elected to aid in the administration of public affairs. In this year the ten original counties were organized. In 1685, on the demise of Charles II, the Duke of York ascended the throne, with the title of James II. This bigoted monarch signalized himself by forbidding the establishment of a printing press in the colony.

Governor Dongan was far better than his sovereign, and

M. J. PAILLARD & CO.,
No. 680 BROADWAY,
NEW YORK,

GRAND HEADQUARTERS

FOR

MUSICAL BOXES.

We are in constant receipt, by steamer, of

FRESH IMPORTATIONS OF BOXES.

Dealers will be able to make a Splendid Selection.

MUSICAL BOXES CAREFULLY REPAIRED.

SEND POSTAGE STAMP FOR PRICE LIST.

NO MORE BAGGAGE SMASHING.

THE

BIJOU TRUNK,

WITH THE

PATENT INDIA RUBBER SHIELDS,

Is the only Trunk yet introduced that cannot be smashed. They are light, beautifully arranged, and perfectly water-proof.

MANUFACTURED AND SOLD ONLY BY

J. C. GILLMORE,

No. 26 FOURTH AVENUE,

Below Eighth Street,   NEW YORK.

at length was recalled, in consequence of his remonstrances against other arbitrary measures he was instructed to carry out with regard to the confederate Indian tribes and the Jesuits. Andros was appointed to supercede him, but his also was but a short reign, for the populace grew disaffected, and, in a civil commotion one Jacob Leisler, a Dutch merchant, was proclaimed leader, and ultimately invested with the reigns of government.

He also summoned a convention of deputies from those portions of the province over which his influence extended. This convention levied taxes and adopted other measures for the temporary government of the colony, and thus, for the first time in its existence, was the colony of New York under a free government. The strong prejudices, however, which had been awakened by Leisler's measures soon produced in the minds of his adversaries a rancorous bitterness which was, perhaps, never surpassed in the annals of any political controversy.

This condition of things existed for nearly two years. To the horrors of civil commotion were added the miseries of hostile invasion by the French in Canada.

The earliest dawn of intellectual light—for the diffusion of popular intelligence had been heretofore wholly neglected—was the establishment of a free grammar school in 1702. In 1725 the first newspaper made its appearance, and four years later the city received the donation of a Public Library of 1,642 volumes from England. In 1732, a Public Classical Academy was founded by law; and with the advance of general intelligence came a higher appreciation of popular rights. But New York was destined to be convulsed by a series of commotions; and among them, the memorable one known as the Negro Plot, which resulted in a great destruction of life.

The trade of New York increased. Her ships were already seen in many foreign ports; neither Boston nor Philadelphia

R. H. MACY & CO.,

14th Street and  6th Avenue,

NEW YORK.

IMPORTERS AND DEALERS IN

Embroideries and Lace Goods,

RIBBONS AND MILLINERY GOODS,

Crockery and Glassware, Silver Plated Ware,

TIN, IRON AND WOODEN WARE,

Ladies', Gents' and Children's FURNISHING GOODS,

HOSIERY AND UNDERWEAR.

Picnic Goods, consisting of Boxed, Canned and Bottled Fruits, Fish, Vegetables, Pickles, &c.
White Goods, Sheetings, Shirtings, Linens, and *Housekeeping* generally.

FANCY GOODS,

Consisting of Bronzes, Opera Glasses, Opera Fans, Jewelry, &c.

Toilet Articles, consisting of a full assortment *Combs, Brushes;* also, *Soaps, Pomades, Lubin's* and *Atkinson's Extracts, Colognes,* &c.
Toys and Dolls and *Doll Articles,* the largest assortment in the country.

KID GLOVES.

The *LA FORGE Kid* a specialty. 1, 2, 3, 4, 5 and 6 buttons. *2* buttons, *98* cents; every pair warranted not to rip or tear.

Goods packed and delivered to all parts of the world; and in New York City, Brooklyn, Jersey City, and Hoboken free.

surpassed her in the extent of her commercial operations. Provisions, linseed oil, furs, lumber, and iron, were the principal exports. From 1749 to 1750 two hundred and eighty-six vessels left New York, with cargoes principally of flour and grain. In 1755 nearly thirteen thousand hogsheads of flax seed were shipped abroad.

The relations of the colonies with the mother country were assuming a serious aspect. In 1765 a congress of delegates met at New York, and prepared a declaration of their rights and grievances. The arrival of the stamped paper, so notorious in the colonial annals of America, towards the end of this year, marked the commencement of a series of explosions that were not to terminate until the city and colony of New York, in common with the other colonies, were forever rent from the dominion of Great Britain. The non-importation agreements of the merchants of New York and other places, in 1768, were followed by stringent measures on the part of the British government.

On the 28th of June, 1776, the British army and fleet, which had been driven from the city and harbor of Boston, entered the southern bay of New York. The troops were landed on Staten Island. On the 22d of August, the British forces crossed the narrows and encamped near Brooklyn, where the American army was stationed. The battle of Long Island ensued, in which, owing to unfortunate circumstances, the American army was entirely defeated. Washington, with consummate skill, crossed the river the succeeding night without observation; but the previous disasters, and the subsequent landing of the British troops at Kip's Bay, rendered it impossible to save the city.

For eight years New York was the head-quarters of the British troops, and the prison house of American captives. Public buildings were despoiled, and churches converted into hospitals and prisons. A fire in 1776 sweeping along both

HOTEL ANNUNCIATORS.

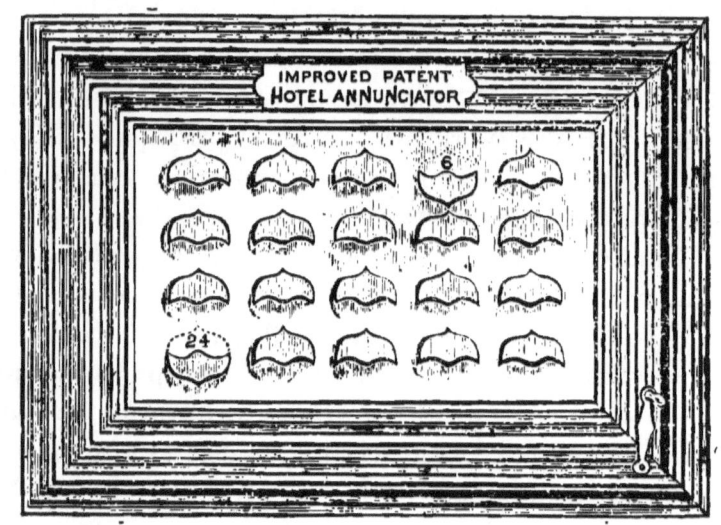

Burglar & Fire Alarms,

Bell Hanging, and Bell Hangers' Materials,

BUILDERS' HARDWARE,

Gold, Silver and Nickel Platers.

MANUFACTURERS OF

PATENT SLIDING DOOR SHEAVES,

Patent Torsion Door Spring Butts,

DECORATIVE BRONZE HARDWARE.

NEWMAN & CAPRON,

MANUFACTORY,
157, 159, 161 West 29th St.

OFFICE,
1172 Broadway.

sides of Broadway, destroyed one-eighth the buildings of New York.

On the 25th of November, 1783, the forces of Great Britain evacuated the city, and Washington and the Governor of the State made a public and triumphal entry.

This important national event, forming the brightest day in the American calendar, is annually celebrated with appropriate military pomp and parade.

In ten years after the war of independence, New York had doubled its inhabitants. Yet the city had repeatedly suffered from the scourge of the yellow fever, from calamitous fires, etc. Notwithstanding all, its commercial enterprise has been rapidly and largely increasing, while its shipping has gallantly spread over every sea, and won the admiration of the world. The first establishment of regular lines of packets to Europe originated with New York, and it is also claimed for her the honor of the first experiments in steam navigation.

Improvements hitherto had been principally connected with foreign commerce. But an impulse was now to be given to inland trade by the adoption of an extensive system of canal navigation. Several smaller works were cast into the shade by the completion of the gigantic Erie Canal, in 1825. The union of the Atlantic with the lakes was announced by the firing of cannon along the whole line of the canal and of the Hudson, and was celebrated at New York by a magnificent aquatic procession, which to indicate more clearly the navigable communication that had been opened, deposited in the ocean a portion of the waters of Lake Erie.

Municipal history is a narrative of alternate successes and reverses. For many years nothing had occurred to mar the prosperity of the city. Again misfortune came. In 1832 the Asiatic cholera appeared, and 4,360 persons fell victims to the disease. This calamity had scarcely passed, when the great fire of 1835 destroyed, in one night, more than 600

OCULIST.   OPTICIAN.

Over 30 Years.

SPECIALIST IN SPECTACLES AND EYE GLASSES!!

BRAZILIAN PEBBLES, CROWN and FLINT GLASS, of the purest quality, mounted in Gold, Silver, Steel, and Shell.

TELESCOPES;
Field,
Marine, Tourists'
AND
Opera Glasses
IN
ENDLESS VARIETY.

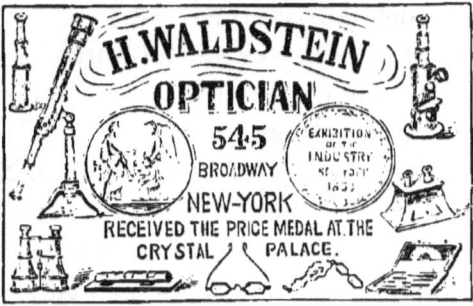

Philosophical
AND
Meteorological
Instruments
OF THE
BEST QUALITY.

The most peculiar Eye fitted with Glasses.

ASTRONOMICAL TELESCOPES.

Particular attention is called to the fine stock of the choicest selection. Strangers respectfully invited. *POPULAR PRICES.*

RUFUS SMITH,

663 Broadway,

Opposite Bond St.

SHIRTS,

MADE TO ORDER

On a New System, insuring a Perfect Fit.

Six New York Mills, ... $18 00
Six Wamsutta, ... 15 00

ALSO,

GENTS' FINE FURNISHING GOODS.

buildings, and property to the value of $20,000,000. The city had not recovered from the effects of this disaster, when the commercial revulsions of 1836 and 1837 shook public and private credit to their centre, and involved many of the most wealthy houses of New York in hopeless bankruptcy.

The completion of the Croton Aqueduct, in 1842, removed the inconvenience of a deficiency of water, and left an imperishable monument to the glory of New York.

A temporary check to the progress of the city was sustained by the great fire of 1845, which destroyed property to the extent of about $7,000,000; but shortly afterwards a new and vigorous impulse was again given to the commercial enterprise of the metropolis by the constant influx of gold from the seemingly exhaustless resources of the *El Dorado* of the Pacific.

HISTORICAL LOCALITIES.

The denizens of New York are such utilitarians that they have sacrificed to the shrine of Mammon almost every relic of the olden time. The feeling of veneration for the past, so characteristic of the cities of the Old World, is lamentably deficient among the people of the New. Still, as there are some who may take an interest in knowing even the sites of memorable historic places of the city, we will briefly refer to some of them. Few, we presume, are not patriotic enough to gaze with interest as they pass through Franklin Square, on the site of the old town mansion of Washington, which stood at the north-east angle of Franklin square and Pearl Street, or tread the sod of Fort Greene, Brooklyn, that battle-ground of the Martyrs of Liberty.

Taking the Battery as a starting point, the first object of historic interest we encounter is the old Kennedy House, No. 1 Broadway. During the war of independence it was succes-

174
5th AVENUE,
Bet. 22d & 23d Sts.,
NEW YORK.

EXTRA QUALITY.

None genuine without the above Trade Mark.

589
BROADWAY,
Opp. Metropolitan,
NEW YORK.

HATTERS.

Authorized Agents in all the principal Cities for our Celebrated New York Hats.

Introducers of Fashion,

AND

MANUFACTURERS OF SILK, BEAVER, CASSIMERE, FELT, STRAW AND OPERA HATS.

IMPORTERS OF ENGLISH HATS.

Agents for { CHRISTY & CO., LINCOLN, BENNETT & CO., H. MELTON, } London.

Sole Agents in the United States for MARTIN'S celebrated

LONDON UMBRELLAS AND WALKING STICKS.

Manufactory and Wholesale Department, 132 Mercer Street.

sively the residence of Lord Cornwallis, General Clinton, Lord Howe, and General Washington. This house was erected in 1760 by Hon. Captain Kennedy, who returned to England prior to the Revolution. It subsequently came into the possession of his youngest son, from whom it ultimately passed into that of the late Nathaniel Prime. Talleyrand passed some time under its roof.

From this house anxious eyes watched the destruction of the statue of George III, in the Bowling Green; and a few years afterwards other eyes saw, from its windows, the last soldiers of that king passing forever from our shores. Still later, others looked sadly on the funeral of Fulton, who died in a house which had been built in what was once the garden.

Here Arnold concerted his treasonable project with Andre at the Clinton's—his head-quarters at the time. Arnold also occupied more frequently the third house from the Battery, in Broadway. Arnold is said to have had a sentinel at his door. When his traitorous character had become known, he used to be saluted in the streets by the epithet of "the traitor-general." He was guarded by an escort from Sir Henry Clinton. General Gage's head-quarters in 1765 was the small low building since known as the Atlantic Garden.

The Bowling Green was originally inclosed, in 1732, "with walks therein for the beauty and ornament of said street, as well as for the sports and delight of the inhabitants of the city."

In 1697 it was resolved, "that the lights be hung out in the dark time of the moon within this city, and for the use of the inhabitants; and that every 7th house do hang a a lantern and a candle in it."

The site of the old Government House is now occupied by a range of dwelling-houses, at the south side of the inclosure called the Bowling Green. It was subsequently used as the Custom House (from 1790 to 1815), when it was taken down.

CANE SEATS BREAK.   EUREKAS NEVER FAIL.

THE EUREKA CHAIR SEAT CO.,
No. 110 BOWERY,
MANUFACTURERS OF

THE EUREKA CHAIR SEAT,
The Cheapest, Handsomest and Most Durable Seat in the Market.

SALESROOM: 110 BOWERY.

MANUFACTURERS OF PATENT BRACE CHAIRS,
For Office, Sitting and Dining Room, Parlor, Nursery, &c.

A FULL ASSORTMENT OF GARDNER'S THREE-PLY VENEER SEATS,
AND CHAIRS WITH CONTINUOUS SEAT AND BACK,
AT LOWEST PRICES.

No. 33. Sewing Rocker.   No. 21. Dining.

Earlier recollections even belong to this location; here the Dutch and English forts were erected. At the corner of Wall and William streets, now the Bank of New York, once stood the statue of William Pitt. The old Stadt Huys stood at Coenties Slip. On the site of the present U. S. Treasury was situated the Town Hall, or "Congress Hall," which included also the Law Courts and Prison. In front of this building were the stocks, a pillory, and a whipping post. This edifice was subsequently converted into a hall of legislature.

It was in its gallery on Wall street, in April, 1789, that General Washington was inaugurated the first President of the United States. This important public ceremony took place in the open gallery in front of the Senate Chamber, in the view of an immense concourse of citizens. There stood Washington invested with a suit of dark silk velvet of the old cut, steel-hilted small-sword by his side, hair in bag and full powdered, in black silk hose, and shoes with silver buckles, as he took the oath of office to Chancellor Livingston. Dr. Duer thus describes the scene of the inauguration:—

"This auspicious ceremony took place under the portico of Federal Hall, upon the balcony in front of the Senate Chamber, in the immediate presence of both Houses of Congress, and in full view of the crowds that thronged the adjacent streets. The oath was administered by Chancellor Livingston, and when the illustrious chief had kissed the Book, the Chancellor, with a loud voice proclaimed, 'Long live George Washington, President of the United States.' Never shall I forget the thrilling effect of the thundering cheers which broke forth, as from one voice, peal after peal, from the assembled multitude. Nor was it the voices alone of the people that responded to the announcement; their hearts beat in unison with the echoes resounding through the distant streets; and many a tear stole down the rugged cheeks of the hardiest of the spectators, as well I noted

POSTPONEMENTS IMPOSSIBLE.

$20.00

WILL BUY A

FIRST MORTGAGE PREMIUM BOND

OF THE

INDUSTRIAL EXHIBITION CO.,

NEW YORK.

Authorized by the Legislature of the State of New York.

FOUR DRAWINGS ANNUALLY.

CAPITAL PREMIUM,

$100,000.

Address for Bonds and Full particulars,

MORGENTHAU, BRUNO & Co.,

Financial Agents,

No. 23 PARK ROW,

P. O. Drawer 29.   NEW YORK.

Applications for agencies received.

Hon. F. A. ALBERGER, Pres't.
W. C. MOORE, Treas.
R. J TODD, Sec'y.

from my station in an upper window of the neighboring house of Colonel Hamilton."

Washington's farewell interview with his officers took place at France's Tavern, corner of Pearl and Broad streets.

New York is noted for its pageants and processions. That on the occasion of the last visit of General Lafayette presented the most imposing spectacle of its time.

In ancient times boats were used to convey passengers across Pearl street. Canal and Cliff streets derive their names from a like circumstance. The Old Dutch records show that the outskirts of the town were divided into farms, called "Bouwerys;" from this fact the Bowery derived its name.

The hills were sometimes precipitous, as from Beekman and Peck's hills, and in the neighborhood of Pearl, Beekman, and Ferry streets, and from the middle Dutch Church, in Nassau street, down to Maiden lane; and sometimes gradually sloping, as on either hills along the line of the water coursing through Maiden lane.

When Hamilton acted as Secretary of the Treasury, he wrote the "Federalist" at a house in Wall street, between Broad and William streets, its site being now occupied by the Mechanic's Bank. His last residence was the Grange, at Bloomingdale. He also lived for some time at Bayard House, on the banks of the North River. The location where his hapless duel with Burr occurred, near Weehawken, is pointed out to visitors; a stone marks the spot where Hamilton fell.

Leisler and Milbourne, the proto-martyrs of popular liberty in America, met with a sanguinary death, May 16th, 1691, on the verge of Beekman's swamp near the spot where the Sun Building now stands.

Where Catharine street now stands was the spot where the stamps were burnt, at the dead of night by citizens, in the year 1776.

BLOOM'S,
338 & 340 Bowery.

GRAND DISPLAY OF PARISIAN and BERLIN NOVELTIES,

IN

Laces,	Velvets,	Fans, Gloves,
Passementeries,	Hats, Bonnets,	Hosiery,
Ribbons,	Flowers, Feathers,	Sleeveless Jackets,
Silk, Satin,	French Jewelry,	Polonaises,

Overskirts, Ladies', Children's and Infants' Outfits, etc., etc.

Their prices will suit the most economical. An early call is respectfully solicited. Samples and Price-Lists sent on application. Goods sent to all parts of the country, C. O. D.

I. BLOOM & BRO.,

Bet. Bond and Great Jones Sts.,   338 & 340 Bowery.

RUSSIAN TURKISH BATHS,
GIBSON'S BUILDINGS,
Cor. Broadway and 13th St.

These Baths are the largest and most complete in this city. They combine the best features of the two most noted and valuable systems of bathing—the *Russian and Turkish*. The *Russian*, in the application of vapor, and the manner of cleansing the skin, together with a series of douches and plunges, thus effecting relaxation and reaction, producing a powerful and invigorating effect; the *Turkish*, in the luxurious shampooing of the whole body.

The use of cold water does not involve such violent shocks as is generally supposed. There is no discomfort attending the process, but, on the contrary, the sensations produced are of so pleasing a nature as to render these baths the means of real luxury.

HOURS OF BATHING:
From 7 A. M. to 9 P. M., and on SUNDAYS from 7 A. M. to 12 M.

DAYS FOR LADIES:
MONDAYS, WEDNESDAYS, and SATURDAYS, from 9 A. M. to 1 P. M.

Single Bath	$1 00
Six Tickets	5 00
Fifteen Tickets	10 00
Quarterly Subscriptions	15 00

Benjamin Franklin, while residing in New York used, as an observatory for experimenting on electricity, the steeple of the old Dutch Church, lately the Post Office, in Nassau street. Who will not gaze with interest at this starting point of that luminous train which now encircles the globe, and by which we communicate in letters of light with our antipodes, almost with the celerity of thought.

The old City Hall, in Broadway, the site of which is now occupied by a row of brown stone buildings, was for a long time the most notable edifice of the kind in the city. Here Washington, with his suite, attended the brilliant assemblies of his days.

A still more interesting relic of the past was the old Sugar-House Prison, which, till within a very few years, stood in Liberty street, adjacent to the Dutch Church, lately the Post Office. It was founded in 1689, and occupied as a sugar refining factory till 1777, when Lord Howe converted it into a place of confinement for American prisoners.

The old Walton House, in Pearl street, was one of the memorabilia of New York City. This celebrated mansion was erected in 1754, by Walton, a wealthy English merchant. It continued in possession of the family during the Revolutionary war, and was the scene of great splendor and festivity.

Washington's city mansion stood at the junction of Main and Pearl streets, the northern angle of Franklin Square. Here the General was accustomed to hold state levees.

The old Brewery at the Five Points, recently taken down, is deserving of some notice. Its purlieus were those of wretchedness and crime; they have been fitly described as "an exhibition of poverty without a parallel—a scene of degradation too appalling to be believed, and too shocking to be disclosed; where you find crime without punishment, disgrace without shame, sin without compunction, and death without hope."

HUMAN HAIR GOODS.

L. SHAW,

No. 364 BOWERY, corner FOURTH ST.,
BRANCH STORE,
No. 345 SIXTH AVENUE, bet. 21st and 22d Sts., New York,
UP STAIRS, OVER MILLINERY STORE.

The only establishment where the largest stock of Human Hair Goods is positively retailed at wholesale prices.
In all cases full satisfaction guaranteed or goods returnable.

PRICE LIST.

Short Hair Switches, 50 Cents and upwards. Switches One Yard Long, $2.00.
FIRST QUALITY HAIR SWITCHES, SOLID, NOT DYED, EXCELLENT FOR WEAR.

Three Stems, 20 in., 1¼ oz..........$1 50	All long Hair, 18 in., 2 oz..........$2 50
" 24 " 2 " 2 00	" 22 " 3 " 4 00
" 28 " 3 " 3 00	" 26 " 4 " 6 00
" 32 " 4 " 4 00	" 32 " 5 " 9 00

HAIR SWITCHES MADE OF THE FINEST QUALITY FRENCH HAIR, SOLID, NOT DYED.

Three Stems, with a coverment of 18 inches long, Hair 4 oz. weight..........$5 00
"   "   "   "   22 "   "   "   4 "   " 6 00
"   "   "   "   26 "   "   "   4 "   " 8 00
"   "   "   "   32 "   "   "   4 "   " 10 00

HAIR SWITCHES made of the finest quality FRENCH HAIR, SOLID, NOT DYED. ALL LONG HAIR.

18 in. long, per oz., including workmanship, $2 25 | 26 in. long, per oz., including workmanship, $3 75
22 "   "   "   "   "   3 00 | 32 "   "   "   "   "   5 00

CURLS Warranted Naturally Curly.
LONG SINGLE CURLS WARRANTED NATURALLY CURLY.

16 inches long..........$1 00	26 inches long..........$4 00
18 " 1 50	28 " 5 00
22 " 2 00	32 " 7 50
24 " 2 50	36 " 10 00

OUR ASSORTMENT AND QUALITY OF CURLS IS UNPRECEDENTED.

COMBINGS MADE UP,
25 and 50 cents per ounce.

GRAY HAIR A SPECIALTY.
Frisettes, in the choicest colors, at 25c., 50c., and $1.00 per yard.

LADIES' OWN HAIR MADE OVER IN LATEST STYLE.

LADIES' AND GENTLEMEN'S WIGS
ON HAND, AND MADE TO ORDER BY THE BEST ARTISTS.

A PERFECT FIT GUARANTEED.

THE INVISIBLE WIG A SPECIALTY.

No. 1, round the head. No. 2, from forehead to nape of neck. No. 3, from ear to ear across crown. No. 4, from ear to ear across forehead.

Price, according to quality and workmanship,
FROM $10 TO $100.

HAIR JEWELRY IN ALL ITS BRANCHES, as
FAMILY MEMORIALS, WATCH CHAINS, BRACELETS, BREAST PINS,
EARRINGS, &c.

☞ Goods sent C. O. D. by express to all parts of the country. Orders accompanied with Post Office Money Order, or money in registered letters, will be sent free of charge.
A Liberal Reduction made to the Wholesale Trade.

During the past few years the attention of the benevolent has been attracted to this locality, and a missionary station has been erected there under the direction of Mr. Pease. The entire cost of the establishment has been estimated at over $80,000.

The old Methodist Church in John street, nearly facing Dutch street, is an object of antiquarian interest. In William street, about midway between John and Fulton streets, stands a range of modern houses, about the centre of which is the birth-place of Washington Irving.

Old Governor Stuyvesant's house stood upon his "Bowerie Farm," a little to the south of St. Mark's Church, between the Second and Third avenues. A pear tree, imported from Holland in 1647 by Stuyvesant, and planted in his garden, yet flourishes on the corner of Thirteenth street and Third avenue, though but the roots and a solitary shoot remain, the tree having been almost entirely destroyed by a storm in 1863.

He lived eighteen years after the change in the government, and at his death was buried in his vault within the chapel. Over his remains was placed a slab (which may yet be seen in the eastern wall of St. Mark's), with the following inscription: "In this vault lies buried Petrus Stuyvesant, late Captain-General and Commander-in-Chief of Amsterdam, in New Netherlands, now called New York, and the Dutch West India Islands. Died in August, A. D. 1682, aged eighty years."

At the corner of Charlton and Varick streets stood a wooden building, formerly of considerable celebrity, known as the "Richmond Hill House." It has had many distinguished occupants, having been successively the residence of General Washington, John Adams, and Aaron Burr. It has been the scene of great festivities. Baron Steuben, Chancellor Livingston, and numerous other notable men of their times having met within its walls.

BATTERSON & CO.,

AUCTION, COMMISSION, & GRAND CENTRAL

Storage Warehouses,

BROADWAY, SIXTH AVENUE, and THIRTY-FIFTH STREET,

NEW YORK CITY.

J. P. BATTERSON, Auctioneer.

Furniture and all kinds of Goods sold at Private Dwellings, Places of Business, or Store Rooms. Furniture bought, sold, and exchanged. Twenty years' experience enables Mr. Batterson to get best prices for all goods sold by him. Returns the same day if wanted. Advances made, if required. Double trucks, with covers, for the removal of goods to all parts of city or country. "PROMPTNESS AND DESPATCH," OUR MOTTO.

Office, 595 and 597 Sixth Avenue.

THE ADVANTAGE OF THE
ELASTIC TRUSS AND SUPPORTER

Over all others is,

That it can be worn Night as well as Day.

It will retain the Rupture EASILY, even where no METAL SPRING will or CAN POSSIBLY do it It will not CHAFE or ANNOY in the least. It is a complete support to the abdomen, removing entirely the weight or pressure of the intestines upon the Rupture. These instruments cause no pressure upon the spine, as nearly all METAL TRUSSES or SUPPORTERS do. Thus all danger in wearing this Truss, of Spinal Disease or Paralysis, is avoided. It will effect

Radical Cures in most cases, if worn as directed.

Hernia can be cured with as much ease and certainty as a broken limb, but it is as useless to attempt to cure Rupture with a Truss that cannot be worn NIGHT as well as DAY, or one that will not *retain the Hernia completely* and constantly until adhesion is perfected, as it would be to cure a broken arm or leg by stripping off the splints and bandages, and moving the broken parts every few hours; but as a broken bone will begin to knit or heal in about eight or nine days, if held securely together that length of time, so in most, we may say nearly all, cases of Rupture, cures will be effected if the pressure is retained constantly and invariably the same.

THE ELASTIC ABDOMINAL SUPPORTER,
In all cases of Prolapsus Uteri, Prolapsus Ani or Piles,

Will be found to be a complete Remedy, as it effectually sustains the whole weight or downward pressure of the Bowels upon the Womb, Bladder, Rectum, &c., thus curing by removing the cause of all Abdominal Weakness.

ELASTIC TRUSS COMPANY,
683 Broadway, New York.

CAUTION.—Some unprincipled persons are endeavoring to take advantage of the prestige of the Elastic Truss, to palm upon the public an inferior, and in most cases a worthless, instrument under our name. No one should purchase an Elastic Truss only at our office, or of reputable druggists or physicians, or of our authorized agents.

Aaron Burr once lived at the corner of Cedar and Nassau streets, and, after he held the office of Vice-President, at the corner of Pine and Nassau streets.

Cobbett kept his seed store at 62 Fulton street. His farm was at Hempstead, Long Island.

Grant Thorburn's celebrated seed store, which was one of the notable objects of the city in its time, was in Liberty street, between Nassau and Broadway. His store was previously used for a Quaker meeting-house, the first that that society had erected in the city.

The brick meeting-house, built in 1764, in Beekman street near Nassau, then standing on open fields, was the place where Whitefield preached.

On the site of the present Metropolitan Hotel once lived the diplomatist Talleyrand, when ambassador to the United States. He published a small tract on America, once much read; he it was who affirmed that the greatest sight he had ever beheld in this country was Hamilton, with his pile of books under his arm, proceeding to the court-room in the old City Hall, in order to expound the law.

James Rivington, from London, opened a book store in 1761, near the foot of Wall street, from which his "Royal Gazetteer" was published in April, 1773.

Gaine's "New York Mercury," in Hanover Square, was established in 1752; Holt's "New York Journal," in Dock (Pearl) street, near Wall, commenced in 1776; and Anderson's "Constitutional Gazette," a very small sheet, was published for a few months in 1775 at Beekman Slip.

Gaine kept a book store under the sign of the Bible and Crown, at Hanover Square, for forty years. Among the early publishers and booksellers may be named Evert Duykinck, who lived at the corner of Pearl street and Old slip, and Isaac Collins, George A. Hopkins, Samuel Campbell, and T. & J. Swords.

AMERICAN DENTISTRY.

According to the official reports from the late Vienna Exposition, the samples of Artificial Dentistry sent from New York were classified with the highest grade of works of art. The peculiar merit of these productions consists in a process of enameling upon the base of the teeth, and also upon the plate, which forms a seamless gum and roof of the mouth, thus producing the most perfect representation of the natural organs. After perfecting this system the inventor, Dr. J. Allen, was desirous of bringing it in fair competition with all other modes wrought by skillful dentists, both in this country and in Europe. The historical records of this system present the following exhibit, viz.: All the awards that have been made by the American Institute for Artificial Dentistry within the last seventeen years have been granted to J. Allen & Son, in the form of medals, bearing dates 1857, 1863, 1867, 1872 and 1873; also, one from the World's Exposition at Paris, bearing date 1867, and still another from the great Exposition at Vienna, 1873, to J. Allen & Son, of No. 314 Fifth avenue, New York.

CENTRAL PARK.

ITS ORIGIN AND EARLY HISTORY.

About the year 1830 the city of New York started from the quiet and steady progress that thus far had been its characteristic, and, with a suddenness almost startling, took the place, which it still holds, and will continue to maintain, as the Metropolis of the Western Hemisphere.

This change came so quickly that in a short time the entire elements of the city underwent a complete transformation. Business grew rapidly, population came pouring in from all sides, buildings increased, and business interests began that demand which is still unsatisfied, upon the premises used for residences. The city was soon deprived of the quiet gardens and detached dwellings that had afforded an opportunity for pure air, their places being filled by solid blocks of houses and stores that increased the evil then plainly apparent of the want of breathing space.

As population increased it became a settled fact that, for the majority of the people, especially for those of limited means, escape from the city for a little rest or recreation was almost an impossibility. There was no place within the city limits in which it was pleasant to walk or ride; no water on which it was safe to row; no play ground for children; no spot for the weary to rest body or brain in the contemplation of the beauties of nature. The localities accessible by water were too remote, or not of good repute; and to the north of the city, there was only a barren waste, save for those whose means and

World's Expositions.

VIENNA, 1873.   PARIS, 1867.

HIGHEST MEDAL   **HIGHEST MEDAL**
AWARDED   AWARDED

FOR EXCELLENCY IN

LADIES' FINE SHOES,

EDWIN C. BURT,

NEW YORK.

CAUTION TO THE PUBLIC.

Purchasers of **Fine Shoes** will please **notice** that all goods of my make have my **name** stamped on lining and sole of **each shoe**, and are made with the **Patent Protecting Edge**, eleven widths to each size, insuring a **perfect fit**.

EDWIN C. BURT.

A FULL LINE IN ALL WIDTHS OF THESE CELEBRATED GOODS,

Also, a choice selection of

𝔏adies' and 𝔊ents' 𝔉ancy 𝔖lippers and 𝔗ies.

A record of size and measure carefully preserved for customers.

A. ALEXANDER,

North-west Corner   357 Sixth Ave., New York.
22d street.

leisure afforded a private equipage wherewith to enjoy the drives on Harlem Lane, and the Bloomingdale Road.

These facts developed in the public mind a longing for a place where fresh air, grass, trees, and flowers, might be enjoyed with little loss of time and expenditure of money. It was about the year 1848, that the people of New York began to find that something must be done to supply this daily growing want.

During this year Mr. A. J. Downing first gave public expression, through the colums of the *Horticulturist*, to this universal want of a great public park. In 1850 he made a voyage to England for the purpose of observing the progress there made in architecture and landscape gardening, and, finding much in the public parks to excite his admiration and command attention, he again, and more thoroughly, advocated the idea he had already advanced of a Park for New York.

In 1851 Mr. A. C. Kingsland, then Mayor of the city, recommended to the Common Council that there should be prompt and efficient action taken upon the subject. This was the key-note from which the press and people took up the strain, and from that time it was a foregone conclusion that the people of New York must have a public Park, adequate to their wants and worthy of the fame of the metropolis.

After many vicissitudes of a legislative character, and much discussion as to the location, the legislature passed an Act on the twenty-first of July, 1853, authorizing the city to take possession of the ground now known as the Central Park.

The first commission, consisting of the Mayor, Fernando Wood, and the Street Commissoner, was appointed May 19th, 1856; they, desiring advice and assistance in the discharge of their duties, invited a board of seven gentlemen, of which Washington Irving was President, to consult with them upon the measures necessary to be taken to adapt the land the city had acquired to the purposes of the Park.

LORD & TAYLOR,

Broadway and Twentieth Street.

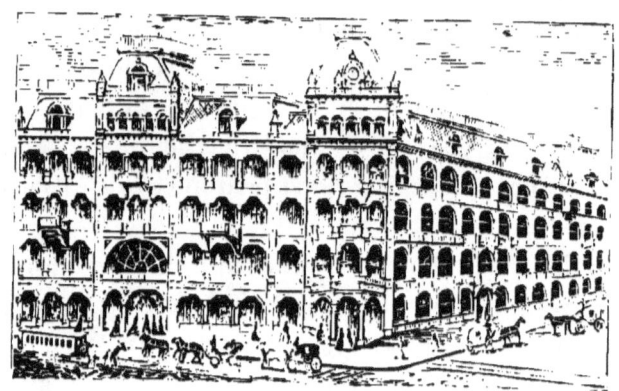

Artistic and Superior Dressmaking

ECONOMY IN MATERIAL COMBINED WITH ORIGINALITY OF DESIGN.

The immense increase of patronage in this department is a sufficient guarantee of our increasing popularity.

THE DRESSES OF

Miss CLARA LOUISE KELLOGG, Madame ILMA DI MURSKA, Miss CLARA MORRIS, Miss CHARLOTTE THOMPSON, Miss FANNY DAVENPORT, Miss SARA JEWETT, Mrs. GILBERT,

AND IN FACT

All the Leading Artistes in the Dramatic and Musical World

ARE FURNISHED BY THIS HOUSE.

All Orders are delivered at the time specified, and PRICES ARE EXCEEDINGLY REASONABLE.

Under this organization a topographical survey of the site was begun, and the outline of a plan of improvements proposed which, however, was afterwards set aside. In April, 1857, the management of the enterprise was placed by the legislature in the hands of a special commission of eleven citizens, under which organization the formation of the Park was begun and continued until 1870, when, under the "New Charter," it was superseded by the Department of Public Parks, under the Presidency of Mr. Peter B. Sweeny. In 1871 this Board was reconstructed so as to contain a majority of the original commission. The first act of the Central Park Commission of 1857, was to advertise for new plans, and on the 21st of April, 1858, a selection was made from 33 that had been submitted: the successful one being the united work of Mr. Frederick Law Olmsted and Mr. Calvert Vaux. The wisdom of the selection is now apparent in the successful fulfillment of the plan selected, which has been carried out in all its essential features, save at the upper end of the Park, where its extension from 106th to 110th streets rendered an entire modification necessary.

LOCATION AND AREA.

The Park occupies the parallelogram included within 59th street on the south, 110th street on the north, Fifth avenue on the east, and Eighth avenue on the west. The entire area is 843 acres, of which 141 acres are occupied by the Croton reservoirs, over 43 acres by the waters of the Parks, and of the remaining space 103 acres are in drives, bridle roads and walks.

The Park is open daily to the public during the months of May, June, July, August, September, and October, from sunrise until eleven o'clock P. M.; and during the months of November, December, January, February, March, and April, from sunrise until nine o'clock P. M. This rule, of course,

LADIES' BOOTS & SHOES.

CASTILIAN INSTEPS

AND

STEEL SHANKS,

AT

TILSON & CHARDE,

635 Sixth Avenue,

Corner 37th Street.

HOUSEKEEPING GOODS.

GREAT BARGAINS IN

TABLE LINENS, NAPKINS, TOWELS,

Linen and Cotton Sheetings, Muslins and White Goods,

BLANKETS & COMFORTABLES,

𝕷adies', 𝕲ents' and 𝕮hildren's 𝖀nderwear,

NOTIONS AND FANCY GOODS.

HOSIERY IN GREAT VARIETY.

J. M. EDGAR, Jr.,

383 Sixth Ave., bet. 23d & 24th Sts.

cannot be, and is not, strictly enforced, particularly during the skating season, and again during the extreme hot weather, when many respectable persons remain in the Park until midnight.

CARRIAGE SERVICE.

Under the supervision of the Commissioners, carriages are provided in which visitors can make a complete tour of the Park. They leave the Merchant's gate, at Eighth avenue and 59th street, and Scholar's gate, Fifth avenue and 59th street, at short intervals during the day and early evening, making the trip within an hour. Twelve persons can be comfortably accommodated in each carriage, and they are not allowed to carry more. The fare is twenty-five cents. Carriages may be procured outside of the Park limits, subject to the following rates of fare, as per municipal ordinance:

"The rates of fare to be charged for the use of coaches shall be as follows: All around the Park, with the privilege of keeping the coach two hours, *four dollars;* principal parts of the Park, *three dollars;* to Casino and Lake, and return, *two dollars;* when engaged by the hour, *two dollars* per hour; when for three or more hours, each *one dollar and fifty cents* per hour."

PARK KEEPERS.

The Park force is constantly on duty, and easily distinguished by the neat gray uniform. Acts of lawlessness are extremely rare within the Park, and the duties of the keepers are almost exclusively confined to giving information to visitors; it being a part of their prescribed duties to give full and complete replies to all questions regarding the Park. The universal public testimony is, that for courtesy and efficiency the Park keepers cannot be surpassed.

Waters' Philharmonic Organs,

in UNIQUE FRENCH CASES, are among the best made, and combine *purity of voicing* with great volume of tone. Suitable for *parlor, church*, or *music hall*.

WATERS' VESPER ORGANS,

in Walnut Cases of UNIQUE FRENCH DESIGN, having Lamp or Flower Stands, Book Closets, with lock and key, and Patent Double *Forte Swell*, beautifully voiced and capable of a great variety of fine musical effects. Are allowed by competent judges to be among the best and cheapest *reed organs* ever offered to the public.

WATERS' CONCERTO ORGANS

are the most beautiful in style and perfect in tone ever made. The *concerto stop* is the best ever placed in any organ. It is produced by an extra set of reeds, peculiarly voiced, the effect of which is most charming and soul-stirring, while its imitation of the human voice is superb. Terms liberal.

WATERS' Philharmonic, Vesper & Orchestral Organs,

in *unique French cases*, are among the best made, and combine *purity of voicing* with great volume of tone. Suitable for *parlor, church*, or *music hall*.

WATERS' New Scale Pianos

have great power and a fine singing tone, with all modern improvements, and are the *best pianos made*. These Organs and Pianos are warranted for *six years*. *Prices extremely low* for cash, or part cash and balance in monthly or quarterly payments. Second-hand instruments taken in exchange. *Agents wanted* in every county in the U. S. and Canada. A liberal discount to Teachers, Ministers, Churches, Schools, Lodges, etc. *Illustrated catalogues mailed*.

SONGS OF GRACE AND GLORY,

The *very best* Sunday School Song Book. By W. F. SHERWIN and S. J. VAIL. 160 Pages, Splendid Hymns, Choice Music, Tinted Paper, Superior Binding. Price, in Boards, 35 cents; $30 per hundred. A Specimen Copy, in Paper Cover, mailed for 25 cents.

SIX NEW SONGS

In pamphlet form for *Sunday School Anniversaries*, from "*Songs of Grace and Glory*." Price, $2 per 100. Specimen Copy of the Anniversary Songs, and six sample pages of the Book, mailed for 3 cent stamp.

HORACE WATERS & SON,

P. O. Box 3567.   481 Broadway, N. Y.

GATEWAYS AND APPROACHES.

The greatest number of persons and carriages enter the Park by the Scholar's gate, at the corner of Fifth avenue and 59th street. The improvements now in progress are rapidly making this gateway worthy of the notable avenue it adorns, and ere long it will be one of the most imposing of all the Park entrances. Its surroundings include an open plaza, on the opposite corner, which greatly heightens the effect, by permitting a view of the Park from some distance down the avenue.

Next in importance, measured by the count of persons and vehicles entering it, is the Merchant's gate, at the corner of Eighth avenue and 59th street, the point where Broadway intersects Eighth avenue, and from which the grand Boulevard runs in a north-westerly direction. To prevent the crowding and confusion that would naturally result from the concentration of so many leading thoroughfares, a Grand Circle, that contributes greatly to the general effect of this entrance, has been laid out directly opposite the gateway.

After those just described, the Artist's and Artisan's gates on 59th street—the former at Sixth avenue and the latter at Seventh avenue—are of the greatest consequence. These two avenues just named are being converted into Boulevards, and will be planted with double rows of trees, thus completing magnificent drives through Park and Boulevard, from 59th street to the Harlem River.

The improvements now being rapidly pushed forward on all the approaches to the Park, with sleepless energy so indicative of the Metropolitan spirit, are arranged with special reference to its attractions, and will ere long form worthy setting of the city's gem.

The names of the gateways have been a subject of much interest, and those selected happily illustrate the fact that

DIRECT IMPORTATIONS AND FROM AUCTION.

WHITE FRENCH CHINA,

AT USUAL PRICE OF STONE CHINA.

DECORATED DINNER, TEA & TOILET SETS,

AT FORMER PRICES OF WHITE CHINA.

Glass, Cutlery, Plated Ware, Parian, Clocks,

BRONZES, FANCY GOODS, &C.

CHANDELIERS AND GAS FIXTURES AT LESS THAN COST,

To close out my entire stock of that branch of business.

CHINESE AND JAPANESE PORCELAIN.

Receiving my stock direct from first hands on the other side, thereby paying but **One Profit**, I am enabled to supply my customers at **Low Prices**.

Decorations on China, and Glass Cutting to order.

RUFUS M. BRUNDIGE,

919 Broadway, cor. 21st.   651 6th Ave., cor. 38th.

WATERS' CONCERTO ORGANS are the most beautiful in style and perfect in tone ever made. THE CONCERTO STOP is the best ever placed in any Organ. It is produced by an extra set of reeds, peculiarly voiced, the EFFECT of which is most CHARMING and SOUL-STIRRING, while its IMITATION of the HUMAN VOICE is SUPERB. Terms liberal. **WATERS' Philharmonic, Vesper and Orchestral ORGANS** in UNIQUE FRENCH CASES, are among the best made, and combine PURITY of VOICING with great volume of tone. Suitable for PARLOR, CHURCH, or MUSIC HALL.

Waters' New Scale Pianos have great power and a fine singing tone, with all modern improvements, and are the BEST PIANOS MADE. These Organs and Pianos are warranted for 6 years. PRICES EXTREMELY LOW for cash or part cash, & balance in monthly or quarterly payments. Second-hand instruments taken in exchange. AGENTS WANTED in every County in the U. S. and Canada. A liberal discount to Teachers, Ministers, Churches, Schools, Lodges, etc. ILLUSTRATED CATALOGUES MAILED.

HORACE WATERS & SON,
481 Broadway, New York. P. O. Box 3567.

Testimonials of Waters' Pianos & Organs.

THE WATERS PIANOS are known as among the very best. We are enabled to speak of these instruments with confidence, from personal knowledge.—*N. Y. Evangelist.*

WE CAN SPEAK OF THE MERITS of the Waters Pianos from personal knowledge, as being of the very best quality.—*Christian Intelligencer.*

WATERS' CONCERTO PARLOR ORGAN possesses a beautiful and peculiarly soft tone. The concerto stop is, without doubt, the best ever placed in any organ. It is produced by an extra set of reeds, peculiarly voiced, from which the effect is most charming, and its imitation of the human voice is superb. For sweetness of tone and orchestral effects it has no equal.—*N. Y. Times.*

THE WATERS CONCERTO PARLOR ORGAN.—We are glad to chronicle any new thing, or any improvement upon an old one, that tends to popularize music by rendering its study either easier or more attractive. Lately our attention has been called to a new patented stop added to the Waters Reed Organ, called the concerto stop. It is so voiced as to have a tone like a full rich alto voice; it is especially "human" in its tone. It is powerful as well as sweet, and when we heard it we were in doubt whether we liked it best in solo or with full organ. We regard this as a valuable addition to the Reed Organ.—*Rural New Yorker.*

AN ORCHESTRA IN THE PARLOR.—The Orchestral Organ is the name of a new Reed Organ recently announced by Horace Waters & Son. The instrument takes its name from its recently invented orchestral stop. The voicing of this is peculiar, producing the effect of a full, sweet contralto voice. Its finest effect is produced when the stops are drawn. Then the full chords are toned down, so that an orchestral effect is given. The case is unique, and makes a handsome article of furniture.—*N. Y. Sun.*

the Central Park is the people's pleasure-ground, common to all, regardless of rank or caste. It seems especially fitting that Youth and Age, Peace and War, Art and Literature, Commerce, Mechanics and Husbandry should be represented in these titles, which will eventually be illustrated by the symbolic architecture of the completed gateways.

Below is a list of the names and locations of the several entrances:

Scholar's, Fifth avenue at Fifty-Ninth street.
Artist's, Sixth avenue at Fifty-Ninth street.
Artisan's, Seventh avenue at Fifty-Ninth street.
Merchant's, Eighth avenue at Fifty-Ninth street.
Woman's, Eighth avenue at Seventy-Second street.
Hunter's, Eighth avenue at Seventy-Ninth street.
Mariner's, Eighth avenue at Eighty-Fifth street.
All Saint's, Eighth avenue at Ninety-Sixth street.
Boy's, Eighth avenue at One Hundredth street.
Stranger's, Eighth avenue at One Hundred and Tenth st.
Warrior's, Seventh avenue at One Hundred and Tenth st.
Farmer's, Sixth avenue at One Hundred and Tenth street.
Pioneer's, Fifth avenue at One Hundred and Tenth street.
Girl's, Fifth avenue at One Hundred and Second street.
Woodman's, Fifth avenue at Ninety-Sixth street.
Engineer's, Fifth avenue at Ninetieth street.
Miner's, Fifth avenue at Seventy-Ninth street.
Children's, Fifth avenue at Seventy-Second street.

THOROUGHFARES.

The regulations of the Park exclude all vehicles of a business character from the pleasure drives; and to obviate the inconvenience incident to the interruption of travel across the city for so great a space, four transverse roads, which are

JAMES M. SHAW & CO.,

Manufacturers, Importers, and Wholesale and Retail Dealers in

DECORATED & WHITE CHINA,

RICH CUT & PLAIN GLASS,

Clocks, Bronzes, Statuary, Fine Cutlery,

— AND —

SUPERIOR SILVER-PLATED WARE.

Hotel and Restaurant Goods

Of the finest Iron-stone China, and unequalled for brilliancy of glaze and soundness of body. Each piece bears our stamp and Trade Mark.

No. 25 Duane Street, New York.

Parties visiting New York respectfully invited to inspect our Retail Stock of

BRONZES AND WORKS OF ART.

JAMES W. QUEEN & CO.,

MANUFACTURING OPTICIANS,

601 Broadway,   924 Chestnut St.,
NEW YORK.   PHILADELPHIA.

Spectacles, Eye-Glasses, Opera Glasses,

MATHEMATICAL INSTRUMENTS & DRAWING MATERIALS,

And Manufacturer of

ALL KINDS OF SCIENTIFIC INSTRUMENTS.

CALL FOR ILLSTURATED CATALOGUES.

carried entirely across the Park by excavations below the level of the ground, have been constructed for the accommodation of ordinary traffic. So ingeniously have these road-ways been located that the visitor is scarcely aware of their existence, and, indeed, a remarkable aptness has been displayed in the arrangement of all the drives, bridle paths and walks, each being so independent of the other that the entire Park may be traversed either on foot, horseback, or in a carriage, without one class interfering with another.

There are nine and one-half miles of drives, varying in width from forty-five to sixty feet; there are five and one-half miles of bridle paths, of an average width of twenty feet, and twenty-eight and one-half miles of foot walks, the latter following all the drives, but leading as well to many most beautiful spots, which are entirely lost to the visitor who only views the Park from a carriage.

THE CROTON RESERVOIRS.

These Reservoirs, so prominent in the scenery of the Park, and so important to the health and comfort of the city, were projected, and one of them completed, long before the occupation of the site of the Park for its present purpose. The Old or Lower Reservoir is a parallelogram in form, 1,826 feet long and 835 feet wide, covering an area of thirty-five acres, and capable of containing 150,000,000 gallons of water. It is divided into two sections, one with a depth of twenty, and the other of thirty feet. Its walls of solid masonry are twenty feet wide at the top, and gradually increase in thickness toward the base.

The New Reservoir was constructed simultaneously with the Park itself, the old one being insufficient for the needs of the increasing population of the city. It lies directly north of the latter, and extends almost the entire width of

FASHIONS. "Smith's Illustrated Pattern Bazaar."

The ONLY Magazine that IMPORTS STYLES and SELLS Patterns of them.
Only ONE DOLLAR and TEN CENTS a YEAR, with a Splendid Premium. See BIG OFFER below.

DESCRIPTION OF THESE ENGRAVINGS.

3019. Polonaise—Very Latest—Stylish—All Sizes—Price of Pattern, with CLOTH MODEL, $1.00.
2018. Polonaise—All Sizes—Pattern, with CLOTH MODEL, 50 cents.
2014. Mazie Costume—Unique—Three Suits in one—Pattern, with CLOTH MODEL, 50 cents.
1307. Lady's Waist—Latest Design—All Sizes—Pattern, with CLOTH MODEL, 50 cents.
2902. Boy's Suit—Sizes, 2 to 6 years—Pattern, with CLOTH MODEL, 50 cents.

2515. Lady's Coat Waist—All Sizes—Pattern, with CLOTH MODEL, 25 cents.
2815. Greek Overskirt—Beautiful—Pattern, with CLOTH MODEL, 25 cents.
1216. Lady's Overskirt—Latest and Most Stylish—Pattern, with CLOTH MODEL, 50 cents.
2915. Sacque Cloak—Surpasses all Others—All Sizes—Pattern, with CLOTH MODEL, 50 cents.
2901. Lady's Walking Coat or Jacket—All Sizes—Pattern, with CLOTH MODEL, 25 cents.

We give a perfect **CLOTH MODEL**, with every pattern, which shows just how to put the garment together, after being cut by the pattern. They are PERFECT GUIDES.

Any Pattern on this page mailed upon receipt of marked price.

Smith's "Instant Dress Elevator."

THIS CUT shows how beautifully a LONG Skirt is changed into a Straight Front Walking Dress by the Instant Elevator. You can raise your skirt while passing muddy places, and then let it fall or you can keep it raised. It keeps the skirt from the FILTH. It LOOPS the skirt in a TASTEFUL and FASHIONABLE MANNER. It saves more than TEN TIMES ITS COST, besides being CONVENIENT, NEAT, and GRACEFUL. It can be changed from ONE DRESS to ANOTHER in LESS than TWO MINUTES. YOU NEED BUT ONE FOR A DOZEN DRESSES. Price, 45 cents each.

WHOLESALE For $2 worth of Patterns at the marked price send $1.50. For $3 worth send $2.25. For $4 worth send $3. The person who sends $3 for $4 worth of patterns, will be entitled to the Bazaar for one year FREE, without premiums.

SUBSCRIBE NOW FOR
Smith's Illustrated Pattern Bazaar,
Only One Dollar and Ten Cents a Year,
And a splendid PREMIUM to each Subscriber FREE!

☞ Any **TWO** of the above patterns and **Smith's Instant Dress Elevator** will be mailed FREE, as Premium, **OR ONE** Dollars' worth of Patterns FREE, to be selected after you receive your Magazine; **OR** one of the following beautiful **OIL CHROMOS**—"EASTER HOLIDAY," **OR** "LITTLE SISTERS," **OR** "MARY AND HER PET LAMB," **OR** the "MATRON," **OR** "UNWELCOME VISITOR." These **Chromos** are widely known, and SELL READILY for from $3 to $6 each, being considered the finest pictures in the chromo art.

GET UP A CLUB!

We will give **one** Chromo extra to the person who sends us **three** subscribers ($3.00 and nine stamps for postage on Chromos and rollers) at one time.
We will give **two** Chromos extra for five subscribers. We will give **three** Chromos extra for seven subscribers. We will give **four** Chromos extra for eight subscribers. Each Subscriber must send **three** stamps to pay return postage on Chromo and for rollers.

MAKE MONEY WE GIVE AWAY $1,350.00 in Gold Coin to 50 PERSONS who get up the largest club for the Bazaar between NOW and First of FEBRUARY. The person who gets up the LARGEST CLUB will get $175.00 in gold coin, AND a PREMIUM on EVERY SUBSCRIBER SENT IN. Next largest, $125.00 in gold coin, etc., etc. We gave $1,000 in gold on last BAZAAR, to 30 persons, whose names and addresses will be found in this BAZAAR, with the number that each one sent. Get a copy and see. Sample copy mailed for 25 cents. "Smiths' Instruction Book," or "Secrets of Dress-making, 15 cents. Catalogue mailed for one Stamp.

Address, very plain,
P. O. BOX 5055.

A. BURDETTE SMITH,
914 Broadway, New York City.

the Park, having an irregular form and an area of one hundred and six acres, with a maximum capacity of 1,000,000,000 of gallons. The summits of the walls of both reservoirs afford pleasant promenades and extensive views, while the skill of architects and landscape gardeners has rendered the presence of these structures a source of satisfaction rather than regret.

GENERAL FEATURES.

The Park is so naturally divided into two parts, by the New or Upper Reservoir, that by common consent they are designated the Upper and Lower Park; this division we accept, and arrange the description accordingly.

It is our purpose to mention only the several points of interest as they are encountered in passing from the southern to the northern end of the Park, and not to follow any special route.

THE LOWER PARK.

This section of the Park is that lying below the New Reservoir, and is the portion upon which the larger amount of labor in the adornment and improvement of the grounds has been expended. The chief features are the Mall, the Terrace, the Lake and the Ramble, all of which, with the other leading points of interest, are noticed in the following pages.

THE HUMBOLDT MONUMENT.

The first object that attracts attention on entering the Park from Fifth avenue and Fifty-ninth street, is a bust in bronze of Alexander Von Humboldt, surmounting a granite pedestal. It is the work of Professor Blaiser, of Berlin, and was presented by the German citizens of New York. The unveiling of this monument, on the 14th of September, 1869,

THE "MOST POPULAR STORE"
FOR
CHOICE NOVELTIES,
IN NEW YORK CITY.

ALL GOODS MARKED IN PLAIN FIGURES.

John Daniell & Son,

IMPORTERS AND DEALERS IN

SILKS,

LACES, RIBBONS, MILLINERY GOODS,
TRIMMINGS,
EUROPEAN FANCY GOODS, Etc., Etc.

Imported Toilet Articles and Perfumeries,

English and German Small Wares,

AT WHOLESALE PRICES,

759 BROADWAY,
One Block below A. T. Stewart's.

OUR SPECIALTY!   BLACK DRESS SILKS.

An extensive Stock of Bonnet's, Ponson's, Bellon's, Tapissier's, Guinet's. Also, other Reliable Silks

MANUFACTURED AT LYONS EXPRESSLY FOR US.

FROM $1 TO $6 PER YARD.

OUR IMPORTATION, THE "ADDIE" KID GLOVE.

In 1, 2, 3, 4 and 6 Buttons, from **98** Cents per Pair upward.

EVERY PAIR WARRANTED.

the centennial anniversary of Von Humboldt's birth, was an occasion of great public interest.

THE STATUE OF COMMERCE

Is appropriately placed near the Merchant's gate, at the Eighth avenue and Fifty-ninth street entrance. It is the gift of Mr. Stephen B. Guion, a native of New York, long resident in Liverpool, and is from the hand of Fosquet, a French artist of reputation and ability.

THE POND.

In the extreme south-eastern angle of the Park, on the left of the entrance by the Scholar's gate, the Pond forms a pretty and attractive feature in the scenery. It has an extent of about five acres, and is partially artificial, being formed to a great degree by the natural drainage of the ground. In the winter season it is the resort of many skaters, as its proximity to the principal entrance makes it more convenient of access than the larger Lake by the Terrace.

THE MUSEUM.

A short distance north-east of the Pond, and near the Fifth avenue boundary, is the old Arsenal, now known as "The Museum." It was formely owned by the State, but was purchased by the city in 1856, for the sum of $275,000. The first floor is mainly devoted to the offices of administration of the Park; the centre portion, however, is open to visitors, and together with the second and third floors is devoted to a collection of prepared specimens of animals, birds, fish, reptiles and shells, that forms the beginning of the American Museum of Natural History, for which a building is now in

PIKE.

OPTICIAN,

518 BROADWAY,

(Opposite St. Nicholas Hotel.)

SPECTACLES,

Silver, Shell or Steel Frames,

WITH BEST BRAZILIAN PEBBLES,

$5.00 a Pair.

OPERA GLASSES.

(ACHROMATIC.)

GOOD KIND.		SUPERIOR KIND.	
11 Lines.	$4 00	13 Lines.	$8 00
13 "	5 00	15 "	9 00
15 "	6 00	17 "	10 00
17 "	7 00	19 "	11 00
19 "	8 00	21 "	12 00

course of erection on Manhattan Square. The Meteorological Observatory finds accommodation in a large upper room, where a number of curious instruments, well worthy a special visit, record the doings of wind and weather. It is the intention of the Commissioners to add an Astronomical Observatory, when the necessary buildings shall have been provided.

In and around the Museum are kept the already large number of animals that form the nucleus of the collection for the Zoological Gardens proposed to be hereafter established. Nearly all these animals have been donated to the Park, and form not the least of its many attractions.

THE DAIRY

Is a picturesque gothic structure, situated directly north of the Pond and contiguous to the south transverse road, which is so connected that all supplies may be received independently of the Park thoroughfares. Here pure milk and similar refreshments, more especially suited to the appetites of children, are supplied at a moderate cost.

A short distance south-west from the Diary is

THE KINDER-BERG,

Especially intended for the use of small children. It has a number of swings and a house with constant attendants for their accommodation. In the centre, upon an elevated plateau, is a spacious vinery, beneath which are walks, rustic seats and tables. Here the little ones may enjoy themselves and not be interrupted by the rougher sports of

THE BALL GROUND,

Which is still further to the west and occupies a space of ten

C. F. A. HINRICHS,

IMPORTER OF AND DEALER IN

FRENCH, ENGLISH AND GERMAN TOYS,

FANCY GOODS,

Glassware and China.

SOLE AGENT FOR

C. A. KLEEMANN'S PATENT ST. GERMAIN LAMPS.

AGENT FOR THE

GLASS FACTORIES of the COMP. ANONYME of NAMUR, BELGIUM.

Nos. 29, 31 & 33 Park Place,   No. 28 Route de Paris,

N. W. Cor. of Church Street, up stairs.   NEW YORK.   LIMOGES, FRANCE.

A LARGE DISPLAY OF

FANCY GOODS

— FOR —

HOLIDAY PRESENTS,

During the Month of December.

acres, also south of transverse road No. 1. Here is a commodious house erected for the accommodation of the players, who are allowed the use of the ground on Monday, Thursday and Saturday afternoons.

THE CARROUSEL.

By the path leading from the first to the second of the above playgrounds, is the Carrousel, a circular building containing a great number of hobby horses which move around a large circle by means of machinery. Here boys and girls may enjoy a mimic horseback ride for a small fee.

SEVENTH REGIMENT MEMORIAL.

On the west drive, near the Sixty-ninth street line, facing the east, stands the latest addition to the Park; a bronze statue representing a private of the "Seventh" at parade rest, of the *heroic* size, designed by Ward. This statue was erected by the members of the regiment as a memorial to the 45 members who sacrificed their lives during the war of the Rebellion.

THE MARBLE ARCH,

Is located immediately west of the southern end of the Mall, and is one of the most elegant and costly structures within the Park, being the only one in which marble is exclusively used. It carries the carriage-drive over the foot-path, which enters it at one end on a level, while at the other a double stairway, leading to the right and left, leads up to the Mall. A marble bench on both sides affords a welcome rest to the weary pedestrian on a hot summer day, and in a niche opposite the upper end of the arch, beyond the stairway, is a drinking fountain.

ESTABROOKE,

ARTISTIC

Photo-Portraiture,

31 UNION SQUARE,

NEW YORK.

Corner 16th Street.   *Over the Bank.*

NON-REVERSED

FERROTYPES

A SPECIALTY.

The Non-Reversed Ferrotype is the finest positive sun picture in the world.

Positions are not laterally transposed.

THE INDIAN HUNTER.

By the main drive, just west of the Marble Arch, is a spirited group in bronze, by Ward, representing an Indian Hunter watching his game, and holding his eager dog in check; farther to the north, at the right of the same drive, half hidden in the shrubbery, is another group in bronze, "Eagles destroying a Goat."

THE GREEN.

Following the drive that crosses the Marble Arch, as it leads to the west and changes directions northward, a broad lawn of sixteen acres, designated as "The Green," is revealed. In the proper season a large flock of South Down sheep pasture here, attended by a shepherd, and supply a simple feature of rural life, contrasting pleasantly with those other portions of the Park where art has done so much to beautify and please.

THE SPA

Is on the north side of the Green, and west of the Mall. The building is highly decorated in arabesque. Artificial mineral waters are here dispensed to visitors.

THE MALL.

The prominent feature of the Lower Park is the Mall, a straight walk which starts from a point just east of the Marble Arch, and extends in a northerly direction for a distance of 1212 feet, or nearly a quarter of a mile. The entire width is 208 feet; and throughout its entire length there is, on each side, a double row of American elms. Comfortable seats are distributed at convenient intervals, and drinking fountains at

GEORGE H. JOHNSON,

PHOTOGRAPHIC ARTIST,

777 BROADWAY, Between 9th & 10th Streets, 777,

OPPOSITE STEWART'S.

FINE PORTRAITS IN

Oil, Crayon, Water Color,

INDIA INK AND PASTIL,

From Life, or copied and enlarged to life size, in the Finest Style of the Art.

With twenty-eight years practical experience on the Pacific Coast and in New York, I am prepared to offer my patrons portraits which in tone, color, shading and finish embody the highest excellence of which the art is capable; and at prices **less than half** those charged by any other **first-class artist** in the city.

Comparison with the best Work is particularly solicited,

and your attention is especially invited to our unequaled specimens of the new Glace and Glace Noir finish, the latter elegant style MADE ONLY AT OUR ESTABLISHMENT.

Cartes de Visite, $4 Per Doz.

LARGER SIZES AT PROPORTIONATE PRICES.

both ends afford refreshment for the thirsty. A statue of Shakspere, the gift of a number of citizens of New York, through the Shakspere Dramatic Association, stands at the southeast corner of the walk, and close by a fine bronze statue of Sir Walter Scott, "erected by his countrymen in New York." At the proper season a number of miniature carriages, drawn by goats and attended by coachmen in livery, are run upon the Mall for the amusement of children, who may enjoy a ride in mimic state up and down the length of the walk, at a moderate charge. The Mall terminates at the northern end in a spacious square or plaza, which is ornamented with two very pretty fountains, and gilded bird-cages mounted on pedestals.

In the summer, when the sun is oppressive, a portion of this space is covered with an awning and provided with seats where visitors may rest. In close proximity to this plaza, and west of the north end of the promenade, is

THE MUSIC STAND,

An elaborate structure, decorated with gilding and bright colors, from which, on Saturday afternoons in the summer and autumn, an excellent band discourses beautiful music.

THE PERGOLA

Is a delightful bower of rustic work, over which are trained wisterias, honeysuckle and rose vines. It is situated just east of the upper part of the Mall, convenient to the Music Pavilion and Casino, at a point commanding an excellent view of the Terrace, Lake, and Ramble.

THE CARRIAGE CONCOURSE,

Is an open square adjoining the Pergola, affording visitors

CITY COMMISSIONAIRE COMPANY.

General Office,

GERMAN SAVINGS BANK BUILDING,

Cor. 14th St. & 4th Ave.

TO THE TRAVELING PUBLIC.

Whenever you need help call a "Commissionaire." He is at all times prepared to do the will of the public in any capacity called for. He will do all errand work for you quick, cheap and faithfully. He will collect your bills, checks, etc. He will find you a comfortable and desirable boarding place. He will secure you seats for the opera, theatre and other amusements. He will bring your valise to and from the depots or steamboat landings. The *professional* Commissionaire will attend to sick persons, paying faithful attention both night and day. The Commissionaires will distribute your hand-bills, circulars, and advertise your business. The Commissionaire will attend your lady when making calls, shopping, etc., acting as "Lackey," and attired in a becoming livery. The Commissionaire will attend your children. The Commissionaire will carry your bundles, bags and baskets. The Commissionaire will carry your baggage, check it, procure your tickets for railroads and steamboats. Interpreters for German, French, Spanish, Italian, or any other language, furnished by the Commissionaire Office. Confidential men for your private affairs, *get Commissionaires*. If you want a man to annoy your bad debtor by repeated calls (three times a day), get a Commissionaire. Get a Commissionaire to wait for your friends at the depot. For a GUIDE through the CITY, get a Commissionaire. And whatever you want (money excepted), get a

COMMISSIONAIRE,

who is ever to be found by day or by night in the thoroughfares of the city, easily distinguished by his gray uniform with red trimmings. Whenever employing a Commissionaire on the street, invariably demand a *check*, else the company will not hold themselves responsible. Ask him, also, for the printed tariff of prices, as we have but one, and no over-charge is allowed.

in carriages access to the Casino, and is a convenient place to pause and enjoy the music of the band without alighting.

THE CASINO

Is a neat and tasteful cottage structure, designed for a refreshment house, where a well-ordered resturant is maintained, and although a private business, like the Refectory at Mount St. Vincent, is still under the supervision and control of the Park Commissioners. It is pleasantly located just at the edge of the Carriage Concourse, and overlooking all the attractions of the Terrace and vicinity.

THE MORSE STATUE.

Easterly from the Casino, at a point near the Inventor's gate, is placed the bronze statue of Prof. S. F. B. Morse, the inventor of the electric telegraph. The figure, which is of the *heroic* size, was moulded by Byron M. Pickett, and cast at the National Fine Art Foundry, by Maurice J. Power. It was procured by small subscriptions from the telegraphers of the United States. The granite pedestal which supports it was provided by personal friends of Prof. Morse.

The statue was unveiled June 10, 1871, with impressive ceremonies, in the presence of an immense audience, including the Professor himself. The fact that this work of art was a graceful tribute from the grateful people to living genius, surrounds it now with unusual and special interest.

"AULD LANG SYNE."

By the foot-path in the grounds east of the Casino, near the main drive, is a group in brown stone, by Robert Thompson, illustrating Burns' poem of "Auld Lang Syne."

Field, Opera and Marine Glasses,

Invaluable to Travelers, Officers, Theatre-goers, &c.,

Compact, portable, and efficient, combining extraordinary defining power and wide field of observation.

EYE-GLASSES AND SPECTACLES
OF A NEW CONSTRUCTION,

Adapted to all defects of vision, improving and strengthening the sight without causing any apparent change, fatigue or weakness, adjusted by,

SEMMONS,

Oculists-Optician. 687 BROADWAY, N. Y.

A New Toilette Preparation.

TO THE LADIES OF NEW YORK CITY:

I wish to introduce to your favorable notice a choice article for the toilet. It was presented some time since to the *élite* of France, my native country, by Pelmaje, the most gifted chemist of Paris.

With a true confidence, which can only be felt in favor of deserving articles, I would thus respectfully invite your attention to it. It is known in Paris as *Destructeur de Rides*, or "Wrinkle Banisher." Its purport is to remove the too premature effects of time, as often witnessed upon the face, around the mouth and eyes, of many ladies. Its use is sure to give strength to the skin and to the muscles of the face when in a state of suspended elasticity. It will be found on trial a most valuable beautifier.

As my knowledge of the English language is limited, I have appointed MADAME GOURNÉ Sole Agent for the State of New York, who will be happy to receive an early visit from any and all ladies who may favor her with a call.

With respect, **MADAME A. MARGETTE.**

MADAME GOURNÉ,

Office Hours, 10 to 4.   101 West 22d St., cor. Sixth Ave.

ALSO, TOILET POWDERS OF SUPERIOR QUALITY.

Although only a few feet from the drive, it is not visible unless approached by the foot-path.

THE BRONZE STATUE OF THE TIGRESS,

May be found a short distance west of the Terrace, to the right of the drive. It represents a tigress, in act of bringing food to her cubs, and was presented to the Park by twelve gentlemen, residents of New York, and is the production of the celebrated Auguste Caine.

THE TERRACE.

Dividing the plaza at the upper end of the Mall from the carriage drive that intervenes between it and the Terrace is a magnificent screen work of Albert freestone, with two openings through which persons can enter the Mall from their carriages, or from it cross the drive to a stairway that leads to the Terrace below. These stairs are worthy of the closest examination, for it will be seen on descending, that no two of the many panels at the sides are alike, and it is their beauty and ingenuity, rather than mere variety, that make them the objects of admiration. The decoration is based upon forms of vegetation symbolic of the Four Seasons, and surpasses the decorative sculpture on any public building in America.

Pursuant to the theory that every visitor, whether walking, riding, or driving, may visit the entire Park in his own way without interference, and to provide another means of access from the Mall to the Terrace, so that pedestrians may not embarrass drivers nor expose themselves to danger by crossing the crowded roadway at this point, a stairway has been constructed from the plaza at the end of the Mall, to the level of the lower Terrace, terminating in an arcade that passes under the drive. The floor and ceiling are finished in

CHAS. EATON
MAN'F OF
OPAQUE & OFFICE
HOLLAND & STORE
WINDOW SHADES
EATON'S SPRING ROLLER AND DRY SHADE.
AMERICAN INSTITUTE
1872
PATENT FIXTURES
WORK DONE IN ANY PART OF U.S. AT NEW YORK PRICES
DESIGNING & LETTERING TO ORDER.
14 PARK PLACE N.Y.
WEATHER STRIPS.
N.B. NOT PARK ROW.

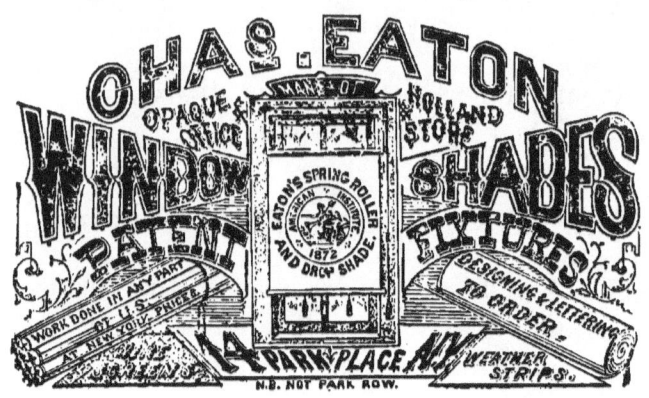

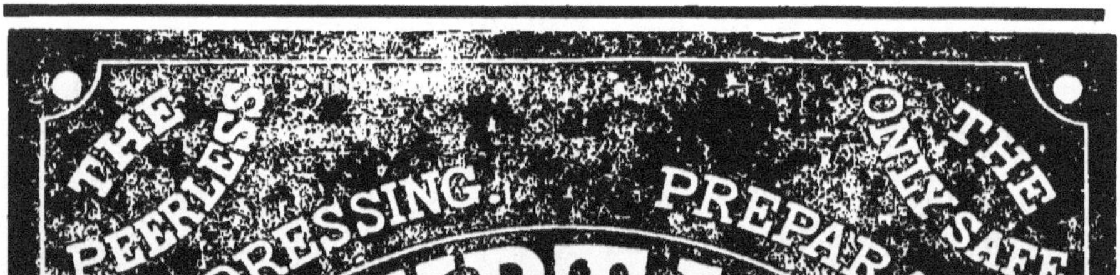
THE PEERLESS HAIR DRESSING.
THE ONLY SAFE PREPARATION.
EGYPTIAN
HAIR
COLORING.
IS NOT A DYE.
NO SEDIMENT.
NO STAINS.
NO POISONS.

elaborate patterns of encaustic tile, and the stone-work is everywhere beautifully carved. The plan for the hall or arcade, for the stairways leading to it, as well as for the stairway from the drive to the Terrace, embraces many artistic embellishments not yet carried out.

Having passed over one or the other of the stairways leading from the upper level, the visitor reaches the lower Terrace, a broad esplanade which stretches north to the margin of the Lake. It is enclosed with a low wall of carved stone which is pierced with three openings, one on either side from which foot-paths lead northward, and one on the water-front whence visitors may take the boats for a row on the lake. At either corner on the water front is a tall mast, from one of which floats a standard with the arms of the State, while the other bears a similar emblem with the arms of the City.

THE BETHESDA FOUNTAIN.

The idea of this fountain was suggested by the well-known passage from the Gospel according to St. John, v: ii, iii, iv. The model for the artistic part of it, comprising the figure of the angel, 8 feet in height; the upper bronze basin, 10 feet in diameter, and the group of four figures below, each 4 feet in height, emblematic of the blessings of Temperance, Purity, Health, and Peace, were designed and executed in Rome, by Miss Emma Stebbins of New York, during the winters of 1864, 1866 and '67. The models were then sent to Munich and cast in bronze, under the able and careful direction of Herr Ferdinand Von Müller, director of the Royal Bronze Foundry in that city.

THE LAKE.

From the Terrace the attention is turned naturally toward the Lake. This sheet of water stretches away from the front

SHOES.

BIXBY & CO.,

8 Astor Place.

E. J. THIERRY,

Importer and Manufacturer of

𝔊ents' 𝔉rench 𝔅oots, 𝔖hoes, 𝔊aiters,

ETC., ETC.

No. 816 BROADWAY,	191 RUE ST. HONORE,
Bet. 11th & 12th Sts.,	Opposite St. Roch,
NEW YORK.	**PARIS.**

A FINE ASSORTMENT OF IMPORTED BOOTS & SHOES ALWAYS ON HAND.

of the lower Terrace to the west and north, in an eccentric outline of bays and headlands, which, with the little islands that dot the surface, the dense woods of the eastern and northern shore, the elaborate Terrace on the southern side, the boats, swans and ducks floating upon the surface, combine to produce a most picturesque effect. It is divided into two parts by the Bow Bridge (so-called from its form), an iron structure which connects the foot-path on the southerly side with the Ramble on the opposite shore. North from this bridge is the Balcony Bridge, which crosses a small arm of the Lake at a point near Eighth avenue and Seventy-seventh street. The swans are not the least interesting feature of the Lake. Twelve of them were originally the gift of the city of Hamburg, in May, 1860. Nine of these dying, ten more were presented from the same source, in November, of same year, to which were added in October, 1860, twenty-four from the Vintners company, and twenty-six from the Dyers company, of London. Of the original seventy-two twenty-eight died, and the remainder with their progeny remain to do the elegant upon the Lake. The swans, and also the white ducks that bear them company, are very tame, and come readily at call. The popularity of the boats upon the Lake is evident from the fact that during the past year no less than 124,000 persons availed themselves of the opportunity for this amusement. There are two classes of boats, the omnibus, which have fixed rates of fare for the round trip, and the call boats that go at the pleasure of the passengers. The boats may be taken at the lower Terrace, and may be left at any one of the six pretty boat-houses that adorn the shores of the Lake.

It is, however, in the winter season that the Lake and other waters of the Park furnish attraction to the greatest number. The care exercised that the ice may be kept in the proper order for skating purposes is fully appreciated by the many thousands that throng to the Park when the "ball is

MURTAUGH'S
DUMB WAITERS

Have now been in use for a number of years and require only to be known to be appreciated. Also,

Hoist Wheels and Store Dumb Waiters,

CARRIAGE AND INVALID ELEVATORS

Of the most approved pattern at short notice.

Dumb Waiters of all kinds Repaired or Altered with all possible dispatch.

JAMES MURTAUGH,

Near 37th Street,   *1370 BROADWAY, NEW YORK.*

up," and when, under a few simple and reasonable restrictions, any one may come and enjoy this exhilarating winter sport. The Scotch citizens of New York find an opportunity to enjoy the national game of curling, on the Conservatory Water. This game is growing greatly in popularity under the encouragement and approval of the Park Commissioners. Commodious houses, so constructed as to be readily removed at the close of the season, are erected during the winter, on the margin of the Lake and other waters, for the accommodation and refreshment of spectators, skaters, and curlers.

THE RAMBLE.

After the Lake, the Ramble is the natural attraction. It covers a piece of ground of about twenty-six acres, sloping upward from the northern shores of the Lake to the old Croton Reservoir, and is bounded on both sides by the great drive, from which access may be gained by foot-paths at several points of the Ramble, although the principal avenue of approach is by the Bow Bridge across the narrow part of the Lake. The Ramble is a labyrinth of wooded walks abounding in sequestered nooks, rustic bridges over little brooks, wild vines and flowers, summer-houses and seats of rustic make, occasional little patches of lawn, all clustering so naturally that the agency of art scarcely seems apparent. It is not surprising that the Ramble has more loving friends than any other portion of the Park, when it is considered how many are the attractions it offers. The Lake shore is beautiful at every point; fine views everywhere reveal themselves; foreign birds, as pelicans, storks, cranes, and herons, have here their home; and for the pleasant chat of friends, the quiet enjoyment of a book, or simple rest from toil, the Ramble has abundant accommodation. More pretentious descriptions than this utterly fail of justice to its beauties.

W. KURTZ,

PHOTOGRAPHER,

MADISON SQUARE,

TWENTY-THIRD STREET,

ONE DOOR FROM BROADWAY.

☞ RECEIVED HIGHEST AWARDS IN

VIENNA, PARIS AND NEW YORK.

BROWNELL & JEWELL
PHOTO-PORTRAITS
889 BROADWAY.

THE MONUMENT TO SCHILLER,

The German poet, is placed in the western part of the Ramble, near the shore of the northern arm of the Lake, and facing the little bridge over the Gill.

THE CAVE.

At the base of the extreme western slope of the Ramble is the Cave, an interesting spot, mostly natural and but partly artificial. A steep path leads to the foot of a large rock, and turning sharp to the left the cave is entered at a level; the entrance is dark, but a few steps reveal the light, and afford an outlook upon the Lake. From the other side, a series of rocky steps lead to the top of the rock over the Cave. A family of owls occupy a niche in one of the deepest crevices of the Cave, and by their sombre appearance and weird looks add to the apparent gloom of the place.

THE BELVEDERE

Is a Norman Gothic structure, situated on a large rock that pierces the wall of the Old Reservoir at its southwestern angle. It not only provides a pleasant place of rest and shelter, but is an excellent post for observation, being the highest point in the Park. It can be approached not only on foot, but also by a "donkey express" that carries the weary traveler to the top of the hill; a species of locomotion much in favor with European tourists, and now for the first time introduced here.

THE TUNNEL

Has been excavated through the rock almost beneath the Belvedere and north of the Ramble, for the accommodation

STATEN ISLAND
FANCY DYEING ESTABLISHMENT.

BARRETT, NEPHEWS & CO.

Office, Nos. 5 & 7 John Street, New York.

BRANCH OFFICES:

1142 Broadway, near 26th Street..........................NEW YORK.
279 (old No. 269) Fulton Street corner Tillary............BROOKLYN.
47 North Eighth Street...................................PHILADELPHIA.
110 West Baltimore Street................................BALTIMORE.

NATHAN M. HEAL,
President.

ABM. C. WOOD,
Treasurer.

NEW YORK
Dyeing and Printing Establishment,
STATEN ISLAND.

Established in 1819.

98 Duane Street, near Broadway...........................NEW YORK.
752 Broadway, near Eighth Street......................... "
610 Sixth Avenue, near Thirty-sixth Street............... "
166 and 168 Pierrepont Street, near Fulton...............BROOKLYN.
40 North Eighth Street..................................PHILADELPHIA.

DYE, CLEANSE AND REFINISH
Ladies' and Gentlemen's Garments and Piece Goods
IN A SUPERIOR MANNER.

of the transverse road that crosses the Park at Seventy-ninth street. It is 146 feet long, and 17 feet 10 inches high, and is chiefly interesting as illustrating the very great expenditure of time, labor, and money which has been found necessary to perfect the attractions of the Park.

CONSERVATORY WATER.

Two and a half acres in extent, lying contiguous to the Fifth avenue, between Seventy-third and Seventy-fifth streets, and a feature of a charming plan, embracing both conservatory, flower-garden, and music hall.

A TEMPORARY ENCLOSURE FOR DEER

Will be found north of the entrance by the Miner's Gate, at Fifth avenue and Seventy-ninth street. It contains several moose and a large number of ordinary deer.

THE METROPOLITAN MUSEUM OF ART

Is now in process of erection on the Fifth avenue side, between Eightieth and Eighty-fourth streets.

THE MAZE

Is located east of the New Reservoir and south of the third transverse road. Within the enclosure are 3,700 feet of gravel walk, and 2,250 trees, arranged so as to render any attempt to reach its central point, or to find a place of exit, somewhat amusing and difficult. When the trees have become sufficiently grown to conceal the paths, the Maze will, no doubt, be a source of much pleasure and amusement, but at present it will hardly repay a visit.

Ladies' and Gentlemen's Garments Dyed or Cleaned handsomely and promptly.

BARRETTS, PALMER & HEAL,
Dyeing Establishment,
DYERS OF
DRESS GOODS, MILLINERY GOODS, &C.

OFFICE,
484 Broadway, N. Y.
(TWO DOORS BELOW BROOME STREET).

Branch Offices:
- 191 GRAND STREET, New York.
- 519 FULTON ST., near Duffield St., Brooklyn.
- 451 BROAD ST., Newark, opp. Continental Hotel.

Col. T. H. MONSTERY'S
New York Salle d'Armes,
619 SIXTH AVENUE,
NEAR 36th STREET, NEW YORK,
For the Learning and Practice of

Fencing, Boxing, Calisthenics, Shooting, &c., &c.

Boxing taught on an unsurpassed Academical System, by which a pupil may become proficient in one month.

A 90-FT. SAFETY SHOOTING GALLERY ON THE PREMISES AND INDEPENDENT OF THE ACADEMY.

A fine assortment of Fencing Apparatus and Boxing Gloves on hand and for sale

Private Instruction to Ladies and Misses in Foil Fencing and Calisthenics.

THE AMERICAN MUSEUM OF NATURAL HISTORY

Is now in process of erection on Manhattan Square, Eighth avenue between Sixty-seventh and Eighty-first street.

THE KNOLL:

Or, as sometimes called, Summit Rock, is in the extreme western portion of the Park, opposite the upper section of the Old Reservoir. Being of easy ascent, its height is quite deceptive; but it well repays the trouble of a visit, as it commands one of the most extensive views to be had in the Park.

THE UPPER PARK.

All of that portion of the Park lying north of the New Reservoir is usually known as the Upper Park, but is connected with the Lower Park by the drive, bridle-road, and foot-path. This section has not received the amount of elaboration that has been bestowed upon the Lower Park, but should not on that account be neglected by the visitor. The special objects of interest are not numerous; but the landscape has a bold, free character, the drives have longer sweeps and stretches, the elevations and depressions are more marked, and the views from the higher points abundantly reward the time, trouble and strength consumed in seeking them. The most prominent features are:

MOUNT ST. VINCENT.

The thoroughfares that lead from the Lower Park pass entirely around a large open space north of the New Reservoir, denominated the East and West Meadows, the roadway on the east side leading beyond to Mount St. Vincent. The

Established 1845.

C. W. CROSLEY,

MANUFACTURER OF

SILK AND WORSTED TRIMMINGS,

Fringes, Tassels, Gimps, Buttons and Cord for

LADIES' DRESSES,

Fringes, Tassels, Gimps and Cords for

UPHOLSTERY TRIMMINGS,

Fringes, Tassels, Gimps and Cords for

PULPIT TRIMMING,

900 BROADWAY,

Entrance on 20th street.

MRS. C. DONAVAN,

French Millinery and Dressmaking.

Imported French Evening Dresses,

NOUVEAUTÉS,

No. 8 East Eighteenth Street,

Between Fifth Avenue and Broadway, - NEW YORK.

building here located was formerly occupied by the Roman Catholic Academy, now on the Hudson, near Yonkers. It is now used principally for a restaurant, where, though the prices are somewhat exhorbitant, refreshments are provided. The former chapel is fitted for the exhibition of the casts of the late Mr. Crawford's sculptures, which were presented to the Park by his widow, in 1860. The basement of this building is fitted up as a museum. Adjoining the Chapel is a fine conservatory, which contains many very rare and valuable plants well worthy of inspection.

OLD FORTIFICATIONS.

Close to the northeast corner of the Park, and forming a pretty point from which to overlook the Harlem Meer, are the remains of earthworks erected during the war of 1812. They have been neatly turfed over, but preserved as nearly as possible in their original form.

THE BLOCK-HOUSE.

Considerable to the west of the earthworks, beyond the Lake and near the Warrior's Gate, which opens upon Seventh avenue, is a small block-house, a relic of 1812, which was used either as a magazine or fortification. This and the earthworks were links in the chain of fortifications that extended across the north end of the island, of which abundant evidences exist further to the west.

THE POOL, LOCH, AND HARLEM MEER.

These three bodies of water are essentially one, being connected with and flowing into each other. The waters flow from the Pool at 101st street, a short distance from the western

JOHN C. HAM,
MANUFACTURER OF
Fine Berlin Landaus,
LANDAULETS, COUPES, PONY PHÆTONS,
AND
Ham's Patent Celebrated Circular Glass Front Landaulet.
I sell 20 per cent. less than Broadway or Fifth Ave. Stores.

An assortment of Second-Hand Carriages taken in exchange, some as good as New.

10, 12, 14, 16, 18 and 20 EAST FOURTH ST.,
One Square from either New York or Grand Central Hotels,   **NEW YORK.**

House Furnishing Hardware,
CUTLERY, PLATED-WARE,
Tea Trays, Fire Irons and Fenders,
CHINA, CROCKERY & GLASSWARE,
Kitchen Furniture and Cooking Utensils,

BRUSHES, BROOMS, BASKETS, &c., &c.

CHAS. JONES,
(Formerly of **BERRIAN'S**,)

920 BROADWAY, corner Twenty-First Street.

wall, under the drive into the Loch; thence easterly in a small streamlet to the Meer, which extends to the northeastern boundary of the Park at Fifth avenue and 110th street. A footpath runs along the margin of the water, and over rustic bridges, by foaming little cascades and quiet pools, to many very beautiful and sequestered spots.

THE GREAT HILL.

This elevation, commonly called "The View," about midway between the Pool and the northern boundary, is a central feature in the northwestern portion of the Park. Its altitude is not quite so great as the Knoll, but it appears much higher on account of the greater depressions about it. There is a carriage concourse at the top, whence there is a commanding view, extending from the Hudson to the East River and the Sound, including a remarkable variety of scenery and interesting incident.

HOW TO GO TO THE PARK.

The public conveyances that lead to the immediate vicinity of the Park, are the street cars, as follows:

Fourth Ave. R. R., from the lower end of the City Hall Park.

Third Ave. R. R., from the lower end of the City Hall Park.

Eighth Ave. R. R., from both Vesey and Canal streets.

The cars of above roads all run beyond the upper end of the Park, thus affording an opportunity to enter by the gates on Fifty-ninth street, or at either of the upper or side entrances.

Sixth Ave. R. R., from both Vesey and Canal streets.

Seventh Ave. R. R., from both Park Place and Broome st.

The cars of these last-named roads do not go beyond Fifty-ninth street.

CHARLES BARTENS,

(Successor to FRED. KIDDLE,)

3 John Street, near Broadway, N. Y.,

FINE WATCHES,

AT WHOLESALE AND RETAIL.

WATCHES AND CHRONOMETERS MADE

And carefully repaired and regulated, and adjusted in temperature positions.

N. B.—The Vacheron & Constantin Geneva Watches a Specialty.

COLTON
DENTAL ASSOCIATION,

Originated the use of

Laughing Gas for the Painless Extraction of Teeth,

And have given it, during the past eleven years, to

77,228 PATIENTS WITHOUT A FAILURE OR ACCIDENT.

COME TO HEAD-QUARTERS:

19 Cooper Institute.

PARKS AND PUBLIC SQUARES

BATTERY.

Situated at the southernmost terminus of the metropolis, connected with the Battery, is Castle Garden. This structure now retains but little of its original past architectural beauty, having been for some time used as a depot for emigrants.

BOWLING GREEN.

Close to the Battery, at the entrance to Broadway, is the small enclosure so called from having been used as such prior to the Revolution. Here stood, at the commencement of the Revolutionary struggle, the leaden statue of George III, which was pulled down and melted into bullets, to be used by the Americans. The railing here plainly shows the marks made by the removal of the ornamental iron globes, that were converted into cannon balls.

CITY HALL PARK

Is an enclosure of about ten acres, containing the City Hall, Court House, and other public buildings, also the New Post Office.

WASHINGTON SQUARE,

Was formed by laying out the ground formerly occupied as a Potter's Field. On one side is the University Building. South Fifth avenue now bisects this Park.

C. H. PHELPS,

WATCHES,

Jewelry & Silver Ware,

677 SIXTH AVE., COR. 39th ST.

Particular attention paid to the Repairing of Fine Watches, French Clocks and Music Boxes.

ONLY EXPERIENCED WORKMEN EMPLOYED.

L. BONET,

CAMEO PORTRAITS,

FANTAISIE,

599 BROADWAY.

UNION SQUARE,

At the upper or northern end of Broadway, extends from Fourteenth to Seventeenth streets. At the south side is the bronze equestrian statue of Washington, and opposite, on Broadway side, stands the statue of Abraham Lincoln.

GRAMERCY PARK,

Situated a little to the northeast of the above, is a select and beautiful enclosure on a smaller scale. This Park is private property, having been ceded to the owners of the surrounding lots by S. B. Ruggles, Esq. It forms the area between Twentieth and Twenty-first street, and the Third and Fourth avenues.

STUYVESANT PARK

Extends from Fifteenth to Seventeenth street, and is divided by the intersecting passage of the Second avenue. The Rev. Dr. Tyng's Church is upon the west side of this Park. The ground was presented by the late P. G. Stuyvesant, Esq., to the corporation of this Church.

TOMKINS SQUARE,

Ten and one-half acres in extent, occupying the area formed by avenues A and B, and Seventh and Tenth streets, is now used as a parade ground, but orders have been issued to place it in its former condition as a park.

MADISON SQUARE,

Comprising ten acres, is at the junction of Broadway and Fifth avenue. On the west side stands the monument of General Worth.

STICH & BROMBERG,

DEALERS IN

Fur, Wool and Straw Hats,

39 MERCER STREET,

Near Grand Street.   NEW YORK.

M. CHERRY,

Manufacturer and Importer of

Trunks, Travelling Bags, Valises,

Ladies' and Gents' Satchels, Umbrellas, &c.,

Cabin Trunks and Sea Chairs for European Travel,

No. 592 SIXTH AVENUE,

Bet. 34th & 35th Sts.   NEW YORK.

Trunks and Trunk Covers made to order.   Repairing neatly done.
All Goods warranted as represented.

RESERVOIR PARK.

Reservoir Square is located between the Fifth and Sixth avenues, and Fortieth and Forty-second streets, and has an extent of between nine and ten acres, upon one-half of which is the Distributing Reservoir. The other, or western half, once had upon it the New York Crystal Palace, but since the destruction of that building by the fire of 1858, the grounds have been kept open as a park.

MT. MORRIS SQUARE.

Mt. Morris Square presents the anomalous appearance of an abrupt hill, with thickly wooded sides, rising from the midst of a plain that has no other hills upon it. It "heads off" the Fifth avenue at One Hundred and Twentieth street, and extends as far north as One Hundred and Twenty-fourth street, and its area is over twenty acres. It is the breathing spot of the pretty village of Harlem, and the favorite resort of the citizens.

RIVERSIDE PARK

Situated on the Hudson River, between Seventy-second and One Hundred and Twenty-ninth streets, is a long narrow strip of land, almost entirely on the river slope, comprising some Eighty-two acres, and at present possessing no other than natural beauties.

MORNINGSIDE PARK

Is another newly laid out piece of ground, forming the area between Eighth and Tenth avenues and One Hundred and Tenth to One Hundred and Twenty-third streets. The land here is so excessively irregular that it could not have been, under any circumstances, adapted to building purposes, hence

NEW YORK DENTAL ROOMS,

ESTABLISHED 1851.

A beautiful Set of Gum Teeth, $15.

On Improved Rubber—The most comfortable and closely fitting material worn.

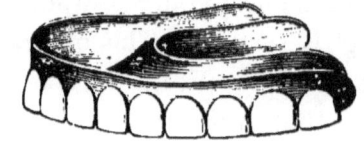

Solid Gold Fillings, $3.

Diploma awarded by American Institute for best specimen exhibited at Crystal Palace, in 1867.

Dr. A. W. MEADER,

Bet. 16th & 17th Sts.　　　　　　　　　262 Sixth Ave.

J. J. CONNER,

311 SIXTH AVENUE, Bet. 19th and 20th Sts.

Manufacturer and Dealer in

FINE SHOES.

CUSTOM WORK A SPECIALTY.

the property owners were glad to cede the ground to the city for a Park, with the view of enhancing the surrounding property.

Under the able control of the present Commissioners all of the above-named Parks have lately undergone a marked improvement. Many of them, more especially the Battery Grounds, were a disgrace to the city, but they are now being fast transformed into miniature Paradises; all have been entirely remodelled, and in some the changes have been so radical that they would not be recognized as the old spots by persons who have been absent from the city for the past five years; Union Square, Washington Square, and the Battery Grounds, are notable instances of the entire and complete changes that have been effected; the most prominent of these, and one that will commend itself to all those who remember what plague spots these parks were after dark, in the olden time, is the removal of the iron railings and fences, and the placing of numerous lights along the paths, making all portions of the grounds as visible as in the day time.

The City Hall Park has lately received a new fountain, which is very elaborate in appearance, though there appears to be a scarcity of water; it has received from the press of the city the name of the "Wayside Cross," though the reason is not apparent, but the "gentlemen of the press" are fond of bestowing titles, both on persons and things, that are inappropriate and undeserving.

THE
Old Chambers St. Candy Manufactory
WHOLESALE AND RETAIL,
ESTABLISHED 1806.

RIDLEY & CO.,
Strictly Pure, Steam Refined

Candy & Sugar Plums,
COR. CHAMBERS & HUDSON STS.,
And 1149 Broadway, bet. 26th and 27th Sts.,
NEW YORK.

ROBERT A. RIDLEY.   WM. KENNEDY.
WM. A. FRITZ.   WM. FORCE.

Zero Refrigerator,

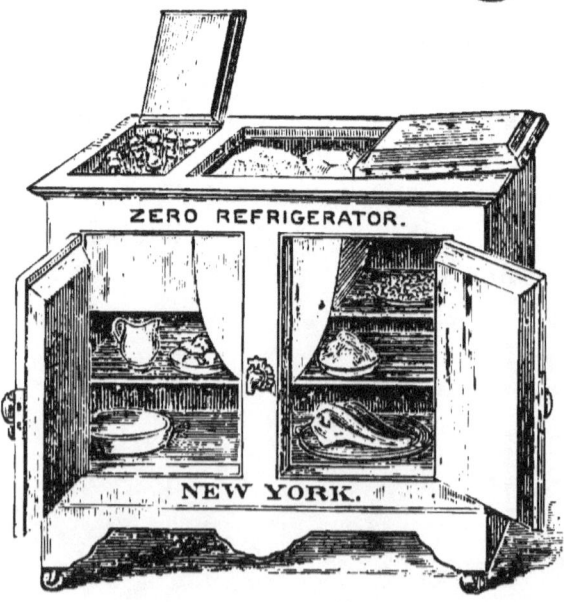

WITH
WATER, WINE
AND
MILK COOLER,
THE BEST
FOOD
AND
ICE KEEPER
IN THE WORLD.

ALEX. M. LESLEY,
Manufacturer,
224 & 226 West 23d St.,
NEW YORK.

THEATRES.

There are no finer theatres in the world than those in this city, and the untraveled lover of the drama may safely content himself with the fact that when he goes to Booth's, Wallack's, or "The Union Square," he sees a stage which London and Paris cannot rival. The Parisian actors are unequaled, for art to them is a second nature; but in other respects our best theatres need fear no rivalry. To go to either of our first-class theatres is like entering a parlor, where only the foot lights divide the guests. The time was in the recollection of our present theatre-goers when scenery was scarcely more than a hint of that which it was supposed to represent. But how different is it now. In the completeness and variety of their appointments our modern theatres are the perfection of art. The scenery is no longer illusion, but reality.

With all this splendor and luxury our theatres combine intelligent acting, and the tendency to make scenery and costume supreme is resisted. All that is now wanted necessary to complete success is a literature of our own; the picture should be worthy of the frame, and the present great want is American plays. Why they are not written is hard to decide. It is certainly not for want of talent, for there is ability enough in every other department of literature. It is to be hoped that it will not always be the case, that with the best theatres in the world, and actors only surpassed by the French, we shall depend upon other nations for our plays.

LE BOUTILLIER BROTHERS

Always have a large assortment of

French and English Dress Goods,

In the Newest Styles, at the Lowest Prices.

SUPERIOR BLACK SILKS, MADE SPECIALLY FOR THEM.
PLAIN AND FANCY COLORED SILKS.
POPLINS, MERINOS, CASHMERES, EMPRESS CLOTH, SERGES, DIAGONALS, &c.
EMBROIDERED POLONAISES AND JACKETS.
RIBBONS, SASH RIBBONS & SASHES.
EMBROIDERED HANDKERCHIEFS, COLLARS, CUFFS, MUSLIN WORK, LACES, &c.
LADIES' UNDERWEAR—FRENCH AND DOMESTIC.
CORSETS, OF THE BEST MAKES.   PERINOT'S PARIS KID GLOVES—OUR COLORS.
HOSIERY, MERINO VESTS, DRAWERS, &c.
LINENS, DAMASKS, QUILTS, SHEETINGS, SHIRTINGS, FLANNELS, &c.

A MOURNING DEPARTMENT,

With all the most desirable fabrics.

48 East 14th St., south side of Union Square.

F. GROTE & CO.,

Turners & Dealers in Ivory,

114 EAST 14TH STREET,

Opposite Academy of Music   NEW YORK.

IVORY FANS, PUFF BOXES, MIRRORS,

OPERA GLASSES, &c.

Repairing in Ivory and Shell done at short notice.

Though there are some thirty odd places of amusement in this city, we purpose presenting the reader with descriptions of only the most prominent and noteworthy establishments.

UNION SQUARE THEATRE.

This celebrated theatre, which in its comparatively short career of three years, under the proprietorship of Mr. Sheridan Shook and the management of Mr. A. M. Palmer, has won its way to the position of the leading comedy theatre of the English-speaking stage, is located in Union Square a few doors east of Broadway.

The very greatest successes in the history of the drama in this country have been won by the enterprise, discretion and tact of the management of this theatre. Their record embraces the successful production and long runs of some of the best of the modern contributions to the drama. "Agnes," "One Hundred Years Old," "The Geneva Cross," "The Wicked World" and "Led Astray," were each of them presented to the American public for the first time at this theatre.

The company is recognized as absolutely the strongest in the country. A glance at the names included in the list will show the perfection of this organization. The leading ladies are Misses Clara Morris, Rose Eytinge, and Charlotte Thompson. The gentlemen, Messrs. Chas. R. Thorne, Jr., McKee Rankin and F. F. Mackay.

The reputation of this theatre for the setting and mounting of plays is more than national in its extent. The most distinguished foreign authors seek to have their plays produced at the "Union Square," confident that their works will receive full justice in the presentation, both from the management in production, and from the company in acting.

RICHARD MEARES,
Sixth Avenue & 19th Street,

Invites an examination of his

LARGE AND ELEGANT STOCK OF

LADIES' SILK COSTUMES,

(Both Imported and of our own Manufacture,)

COMBINING STYLE & ELEGANCE WITH MODERATION IN PRICE.

Elegant Black Silk Walking Suits, in Newest Designs,
$55, 65, 69, 75, 85, 95 and 100.

VERY STYLISH COLORED GROS GRAIN SILK DRESSES,
$75, 88, 95 and 100.

Over Skirts and Basques, Walking Jackets and Polonaises,
Beaded and Embroidered, in latest novelties.

HOUSE DRESSES, MORNING AND FINE UNDERWEAR,
In Linen, Cambric and Muslin.

Ladies', Misses' and Infants' Complete Outfits and Trousseaux
A SPECIALTY.

FINE IMPORTED ROUND HATS AND BONNETS

From the most celebrated Paris modistes; and a large and choice collection of

FLOWERS AND FEATHERS.

Black and Colored Silks and Dress Goods,
Fine Laces and Embroideries,

And a superb stock of

HOSIERY, MERINO UNDERWEAR AND GLOVES,
Much under prevailing prices.

RICHARD MEARES,
Cor. Sixth Ave. and 19th St.

BOOTH'S THEATRE.

This magnificent structure, situated on **Twenty-third** street, between **Fifth** and **Sixth** avenues, covering an area of 200 feet in depth and 100 feet in width, was erected at a cost of $800,000. Constructed of granite, it consists of four stories, with a double French roof. The simplicity of the edifice is remarkable, while at the same time it is one of the grandest buildings in the city, and, perhaps, in the country. There is one grand entrance on Twenty-third street, and one on Sixth avenue, and at the close of the performances, five other means of egress, opening directly on the street, are thrown open to the audience.

The seating capacity of the theatre, including the private boxes, will accommodate 2,000 persons with ease. The auditorium is lighted by electricity. An efficient fire brigade, composed of the different employees of the theatre, thoroughly drilled in the working of the numerous fire apparatus throughout the building, with four watchmen continually patrolling the building, lend additional security, in case of fire, to the easy and rapid means of egress afforded the audience.

Messrs. Jarrett & Palmer are the present lessees of this theatre, and promise a season of unrivaled interest to theatre goers. They have planned a series of labors, in which the claims of dramatic art, the influence of the stage upon society, and the duty of a manager to the intellectual, moral and spiritual needs of the time appear to be recognized. They therefore will command, by serving truth and right, the support of those to whom these qualities are dear. They begin the greatest work of their lives in a sober and thoughtful spirit; they receive with honor the spotless mantle of Edwin Booth, and they open a noble theatre with genuine and practical reverence for the genius of the place.

MILLER & GRANT,
879 BROADWAY, NEW YORK,
IMPORTERS OF THE LATEST NOVELTIES
IN
Rich Laces and Lace Goods,
DRESS AND CLOAK TRIMMINGS,
EMBROIDERIES,
RIBBONS,
Fancy Goods, Fans,
&c., &c., &c.

ATWOOD,
APOTHECARY,
846 Broadway, adjoining Wallack's Theatre,
RELIABLE DRUGS AND MEDICINES,
Physicians' Prescriptions and Family Medicines
Supplied at all hours by competent Pharmacists.

CROWN PERFUMES, Choicest Odors.
CROWN HAIR BRUSHES, Elastic and Durable Bristle.
CROWN TOOTH BRUSHES, every variety of Shape.
Bristles will not break off or fall out while using.

TOILET CUTLERY OF EVERY DESCRIPTION,
Ivory and Tortoise Shell Combs, Brushes, Mirrors, &c. Also, Cosmetiques, Blancs, Rouges, Crayons, Blonde Powders, &c.

FINE CUP AND TOILET SPONGES.
THE ATWOOD COLOGNE,
DELICATE, LASTING AND FRAGRANT.

WALLACK'S THEATRE.

This justly entitled Home of Comedy was first opened at the theatre corner of Broadway and Broome street, where, for a decade, it kept the highest rank as a theatre for the representation of the best school of dramas and comedies. The next movement of the late veteran manager, Mr. James W. Wallack, was to build the present theatre, corner of Thirteenth street and Broadway. This place of amusement was opened in 1861, and was, until the death of the elder Wallack, under his immediate management. At his decease the property became his son's, the present proprietor and manager, Mr. Lester Wallack. This management has now steadily held the first place in the public estimation for a quarter of a century. New York looks to Wallack's Theatre as the pilot and safeguard of the drama—the theatre where the higher and better class of dramatic works finds a permanent home. His company is always selected with a view to the most perfect cast of legitimate comedy. It is very seldom, we can truly say, we have seen a good play badly acted at Wallack's Theatre. In saying so much we do not intend to praise, but to be just. The building is not very pretentious, but is comfortable, and large enough for the purposes intended, and their plays are always admirably put upon the stage. The stock company, at the regular theatrical season, numbers among its members some actors and actresses who would be "stars" at most of the other theatres. The names of artists who have appeared under the Wallack management are the brightest in the list of the ornaments of the stage. Messrs. Walcot, Blake, Fisher, Brougham, Gilbert, Sothern; Mesdames Hoey, Gannon, Vernon, Laura Keene, Henriques, Jennings, and others. As a school of acting Wallack's Theatre is one of the best in any country where the English language is spoken.

POMEROY'S TRUSSES.

POMEROY'S BAND TRUSSES.

These are, beyond comparison, the most perfect instruments in use for the retention and cure of Hernia. They consist of a light, metallic band, accurately shaped to the contour of the pelvis for each case, and so nicely fitted that no pressure is felt, except on the gluteal muscles behind and the inguinal canal in front.

The Rupture Pads are varied in construction, form and size, according to the requirements of each case. The celebrated Finger Pad will effect a radical cure in most cases, without discomfort to the patient.

POMEROY'S ELASTIC RUPTURE BELTS.

These are an improvement on the much advertised "Elastic Truss," so called, and are warranted superior to all other "Elastic Trusses" without metal springs. No person whose attention has been directed to the so called "Elastic Truss" should fail to see the "Elastic Rupture Belt" before purchasing. Price, $4.

POMEROY & CO., 744 Broadway, New York.

ABBOTT'S ZIRCON SOAP

Will wash Clothes in one-fifth of the time; wear one-third longer; gives Cotton, Muslin, and Linen a lustrous whiteness; renders Flannels soft and flexible; removes stains from Table Linen, Napkins, etc.; is elegant for the Bath or Toilet, leaving the skin soft and pliant; takes less than one-half the quantity of any Soap in use.

Warranted not to injure the most delicate Fabric.

ASK YOUR GROCER FOR IT.

WHOLESALE AND RETAIL TRADE SUPPLIED.

NEW YORK ZIRCON SOAP CO.,
No. 1 Barclay Street, New York.

THE COLOSSEUM,

Corner of Thirty-fifth street and Broadway, is a novelty in the building art, rendered necessary by the purposes for which it is intended, viz., the exhibition of the somewhat famous historical Cyclorama of "London by Day," painted by E. T. Parris in 1828, and exhibited in London for over forty years. The painting, covering over 40,000 square feet of canvas, represents London as it appears from the dome of St. Paul's Cathedral, and must therefore be stretched in a circle around the observer, who views it from a great elevation.

There is also exhibited here, besides "London by Day," the equally marvelous and magnificent historical Cyclorama illusion, by Danson & Sons, of "Paris by Moonlight," and the still more interesting Cyclorama, also by the same artist, of "Modern London by Night." In these miracles of art, the illusion that one is looking down from a great height upon an illuminated city is absolutely perfect. The beautiful effects of moonlight, storm and lightning, are presented with such extraordinary fidelity that nervous and sensitive persons find it difficult to preserve their equanimity. The wondrous comparison between London of 1828 and London of 1873, presents an extremely interesting history of the march of improvement in the great city.

The Grand Promenade on the first floor consists of alcoves, elegantly decorated and furnished, affording abundant facility for high-toned intellectual and moral entertainments.

This department is in charge of Professor Tobin, late of the London Polytechnic. Besides the novelties of the Grand Promenade, Professor Tobin presides over "The Lectorium," a bijou theatre, south of the grand entrance, elegantly and comfortably fitted up. Here Professor Tobin

Lock Shank Rivet Buttons.

WARRANTED NOT TO COME OFF.

Inserted on all Shoes, free of charge,

AT THE

EAST SIDE AGENCY for E. C. BURT'S FINE SHOES,

SAMUEL COHN,

281 Grand Street,

Near Forsyth Street. NEW YORK.

CIGARS AND CIGARETTES.

Direct Importation from Havana.

H. LEVY & BROTHER,

848 Broadway, New York.

TWO DOORS FROM WALLACK'S THEATRE.

gives scientific expositions during each day and evening, comprising familiar lectures upon popular subjects of interest, illustrated by an extensive cabinet of philosophical and chemical apparatus, with mechanical and musical effects in endless variety. These experiments and wonderful effects are not jugglers' tricks, or the delusive arts of conjurers, but the combinations and results of scientific knowledge.

Mr. W. A. Lilleindahl, the well known manager, has charge of the interests of the Colosseum.

PARK THEATRE,

Broadway between 21st and 22d streets, is admirably situated in the hotel centre of the city. Mr. William Stuart, formerly of the Winter Garden, is the proprietor, and Mr. Chandos Fulton is the acting manager.

The season was inaugurated with Mark Twain's "Gilded Age," a drama that bids fair to run far into the winter; this success being mainly attributable to the efforts of Mr. Raymond, who has succeeded in making the character of "Col. Sellers" as famous as those of "Rip Van Winkle" and "Solon Shingle." There is ample accommodation for seating about twelve hundred persons, no stools are allowed in the aisles, and every part of the stage can be distinctly seen from all parts of the auditorium.

The Park will be devoted solely to the production of American dramas and comedies, the stage being particularly adapted to this class of plays only.

The orchestra is entirely hidden from view; the effect of this innovation being particularly noticeable in those dramas where music is a necessary concomitant; the pathos of these passages being sometimes marred by the gymnastic antics of the musicians in those orchestras which are arranged in full view of the audience.

IF YOU WANT A GOOD SET OF FURS,
Go to C. C. SHAYNE & CO., Manufacturers.

If you want a good Sealskin Sacque,
Go to C. C. SHAYNE & CO., Manufacturers.

If you want a set of Child's Furs,
Go to C. C. SHAYNE & CO., Manufacturers.

If you want a Handsome Muff or Boa,
Go to C. C. SHAYNE & CO., Manufacturers.

If you want a pair of Fur Gloves,
Go to C. C. SHAYNE & CO., Manufacturers.

If you wish to buy your husband a Fur Muffler or a Sealskin Cap,
Go to C. C. SHAYNE & CO., Manufacturers.

If you wish to buy your wife a set of Furs, or any kind of Fur Garment,
Go to C. C. SHAYNE & CO., Manufacturers.

If you want your Muff relined,
Go to C. C. SHAYNE & Co., Manufacturers.

If you want your Seal Sacque relined or trimmed with fashionable fur,
Go to C. C. SHAYNE & Co., Manufacturers.

If you want Fur Trimmings,
Go to C. C. SHAYNE & CO., Broadway and 10th St.

If you want Furs of any description, go to C. C. SHAYNE & CO., Importers and Manufacturers of Furs, agents for Hudson Bay Company, Broadway corner Tenth street.

Read what the leading papers say in regard to the Furs manufactured by C. C. Shayne & Co.

The Christian Union says: "New York and Brooklyn ladies of the better classes will this season patronize the house of C. C. Shayne & Co., the leading fashionable resort for reliable and elegant Furs. The goods manufactured by this firm are all made from choice skins, properly cured and dressed before being used, so that every article can be fully relied upon."

The New York Weekly says: "C. C. Shayne & Co., the leading fashionable fur house (agents for Hudson Bay Company), corner Broadway and Tenth street, have a splendid stock of Furs."

The Daily Graphic says: "Ladies wishing to see all the leading fashionable Furs should visit the establishment of C. C. Shayne & Co., corner of Broadway and Tenth street. This firm is now recognized as authority on Furs, and have the patronage of the leading families of the metropolis. Their goods are all made up in the latest and most fashionable style from selected skins, thoroughly cured by proper dressing before being used for manufacturing, so that every garment can be fully relied upon as being perfect in every particular. Messrs. Shayne & Co.'s new method of curing and dressing furs has proved a great success.

The press and people all speak in praise of the Elegant Furs manufactured by

C. C. SHAYNE & CO.,
Broadway & Tenth St.,

The firm is desirous of building up a large business, and in order to accomplish the object are offering

DECIDED BARGAINS.

NIBLO'S GARDEN,

In Broadway, between Prince and Houston streets, in the rear of the Metropolitan Hotel, was rebuilt by Mr. A. T. Stewart on the site of the old theatre, destroyed by fire three years ago. The old house was built in 1850, and was one of the largest theatres in the city. It was first opened under the management of Wm. Niblo.

There are very few strangers who have ever visited New York who have not been to Niblo's Garden. For many years the Ravels were the great attraction. Subsequently, the "Black Crook" and kindred spectacles, under the management of Jarrett & Palmer, made this house famous throughout the entire United States. With a large seating capacity the house was thronged nightly for nearly two years with admiring throngs of visitors, while many were turned away from the doors unable to obtain admission. Mr. C. R. Thorne is the present lessee, and inaugurated his management in September, 1874, with his magnificent spectacular drama, "The Deluge." The theatre is devoted to spectacular dramas, ballet and opera, all to be produced on a scale of magnificence unsurpassed by the efforts of previous managements.

OLYMPIC THEATRE.

This theatre, situated on Broadway, between Houston and Bleecker streets, was originally entitled "Laura Keene's Theatre." Built by John Trimble, and opened under the management of Miss Laura Keene, October, 1856. During the period of that lady's management many of the present theatrical stars were in the list of the regular company. When the theatre passed under the management of Mrs. John Wood, it was re-christened "The Olympic."

The auditorium is commodious, with easy egress for the largest audiences, and the stage arrangements are among

MOSCHCOWITZ & RUSSELL,

DRESS MAKING.

NEW YORK,	PARIS,
21 University Place.	24 Rue du 4 Septembre.

ANCIENNE MAISON LAMBERT,

MADAME R. DE WAIBEL,

DE PARIS,

CORSETS, ROBES ET MODES,

No. 27 East Eighteenth Street,

Corner of Broadway.   NEW YORK.

BROWN'S
London Round Hats & Paris Bonnets,

Imported for seven years by

EMMA BROWN,

Sister of W. C. BROWN, New Bond Street, London,

1261 BROADWAY,

Bet. 31st and 32d Streets.   NEW YORK.

MISS GEDNEY,

Between Fifth Avenue and Broadway.   19 West Thirtieth Street.

IMPORTER,

Robes et Lingerie, Coiffures Breakfast Caps,

CRINOLINES, CORSETS, &c.

PARIS DRESSMAKING.

the best in the world. The seats are commodious, affording easy view of the stage from all parts of the auditorium.

Mr. Woolcott is the present lessee, and under his able management the performances given are of the first order of merit. "Variety" is the motto. The programme undergoes an incessant change; old favorites and new talent are being continually brought out; spectacle, burlesque, negro acts, acrobatic performances, opera, are all blended together artistically. The audience have no tedious "waits" between the acts; pieces follow each other in an uninterrupted flow. Mr. Woolcott is determined to make the Olympic the "Alhambra" of New York, and we have every assurance of his success.

ACADEMY OF MUSIC,

Irving Place and Fourteenth street. This is the only opera house, strictly speaking, in the city; was incorporated in 1862, and inaugurated ten years later by Grisi and Mario. The present is the second edifice that has been erected on this site, the first having been destroyed by fire May 1866.

BRYANT'S MINSTRELS.

Mr. Bryant has opened his opera house on Twenty-third street, near Sixth avenue, for the eighteenth season. He has secured the services of all the old favorites, and added several well known in the field of minstrelsy. Mr. Bryant's purpose (in which he has admirably succeeded) is to make his little theatre one of the most attractive of the up-town resorts, and which shall command the respect and attention of the refined and the intelligent. The performances here are always chaste, entertaining and highly amusing. No other entertainment of this nature in the country will bear comparison with that of this organization.

Between Sixteenth and Seventeenth Streets, on the West side of Fifth Avenue, is the

Grand Conservatory of Music,
OF THE CITY OF NEW YORK,

Of which Prof. ERNST EBERHARD is the Founder and General Director.

Although but recently established it has already the confidence of a large constituency.

The system of education adopted in the Grand Conservatory is similar, in many respects, to the course adopted by the leading conservatories of Europe, and is within the reach of the amateur as well as professional student.

It presents all the advantages of eminent professorship, of lectures, of practical public exhibition, of consulting library, and, further, by means of the excellent orchestra attached to it, enables the young composers to study the effects of their maturing efforts in the art of instrumenting for the orchestra—an advantage to the student which cannot be over estimated.

Every department of musical art is represented in its course of study, and each branch is entrusted to the care of a professor of eminence only.

The course of studies embrace :

THE PIANO-FORTE, ORGAN, FORMATION AND CULTIVATION OF THE VOICE, HARMONY, COUNTERPOINT, COMPOSITION, INSTRUMENTATION, VIOLIN, VIOLONCELLO, FLUTE, WITH THE OTHER REED AND BRASS INSTRUMENTS, AND INSTRUMENTS OF PERCUSSION, AND THE HARP, TOGETHER WITH THE ITALIAN, FRENCH AND GERMAN LANGUAGES AND DRAWING.

The Amateur Orchestra, Opera, and Musical Library connected with the Institute, offer great facilities for instruction and concerted practice.

The Artist's Department is kept exclusively for those who design to make music their profession, and are willing to devote sufficient time to acquire the requisite theoretical, practical and intellectual knowledge. The course of study in this Department differs from that adapted to the amateur student ; it is wider in its scope, more exhaustive in its details, and more varied in its branches ; and a more rigid observance of the rules relating to practice is demanded from those who enter their names as professional students.

The regular course comprises one solo instrument or solo singing, with *ensemble*. Also, Harmony, Counterpoint, Thorough Bass, Instrumentation, History, Æsthetics, and one foreign language.

By special arrangement, the pupils of the Artist Department have the privilege of attending the Rehearsals of the Philharmonic Society without charge.

PUBLIC BUILDINGS.

THE CITY HALL.

This is an imposing edifice, and for the most part, built of marble. It was constructed between the years 1803-10, and occupied about nine years in its construction, at a cost of about $700,000. At the celebration of the Atlantic Telegraph, the clock tower and other upper portions of the building were destroyed by fire, but have since been rebuilt.

In the building are the several offices of the Mayor, Common Council, and Aldermen, the Governor's Room, City Library, and other business offices.

The Governor's Room, as it is called, will be a place of interest to many strangers, from the fact that it contains portraits of many distinguished statesmen and other public functionaries—of greater or less merit—and a desk on which Washington wrote his first message to Congress. The chairs used in the first Congress are in the Aldermanic Chamber, and the chair used by Washington when he was inaugurated first President of the United States is in the Mayor's office.

The United States District Court is located in Chambers street, at the rear of the City Hall. The several other Courts are held in the brown stone building, situated at the north-east angle of the City Hall.

THE NEW COURT HOUSE.

This building, not yet entirely completed, is situated in

the rear of the City Hall, on Chambers street, and will be one of the most substantial edifices in the United States. Its equal is certainly not to be found in the city, and the immensity of the structure can only be seen and felt by a comparison with buildings of great capacity, towering as it does above the five-story buildings in the vicinity, completely overlooking the present City Hall, and commanding as fine a view of the surroundings of New York as can possibly be had. It was commenced in September, 1861, under the direction and superintendence of Mr. Cummings H. Tucker, who was appointed by the Board of Supervisors for this purpose. The entire length of the building is 250 feet, and the breadth 150; rectangular in form, and three stories in height above ground. The plans and designs called for materials (particularly with reference to iron and marble) of great magnitude, and the expense attendant upon their selection, preparation, and adaptation, together with all the embellishments, is necessarily very heavy. The height of the new Court House, from the base course to top of pediment, is 97 feet. The dome will be 128 feet high above the pediment, making a total height of the building, from the base course to the top of dome, 225 feet. From the sidewalk to the pediment the building is 82 feet high, and from sidewalk to top of the dome, 210 feet.

The new Court House is an entirely fire-proof building—the ceilings from base to attic all being formed of brick arches—and when we consider that here will be deposited all the records, wills, leases, and documents of the offices of the Register, County Clerk, and Surrogate, the citizens of New York, who are all more or less interested in the preservation of these, will feel a security as to their property and interests not hitherto felt.

It affords accommodations for County Clerk, Register, Surrogate, Sheriff, and Tax Departments and Tax Offices—

departments in which it is of the utmost importance that business should be transacted daily and with dispatch.

The Court rooms are large, airy, unobstructed by columns, made with reference to the principles of acoustics, and finished in an agreeable and pleasing manner, so that they form an attractive feature to the spectator, and all to whom may be entrusted the administration of justice; differing in this respect from most of the large rooms in the Capitol at Washington, the City Hall and other public buildings in which, as a general thing, the shadows and sombre hues are so strong as to intercept that light and heat so necessary to lend a cheerful aspect to any auditory.

THE HALL OF RECORDS,

Located to the east of the City Hall, was originally used for a prison, and subsequently as a cholera hospital. It is of coarse stone stuccoed over; the entrances north and south are ornamented with Ionic columns. The building is now used as the Depository for Deeds, Records, etc.

THE HALLS OF JUSTICE.

This is the city prison, or as it is more familiarly styled, from its gloomy aspect, "The Tombs." It is a spacious building, or rather series of buildings, occupying the square bounded by Centre street on the east, Elm street on the west, and Franklin and Leonard streets on the north and south. It is a massive structure in the Egyptian style, the main entrance being by an ascent of steps beneath a large portico supported by massive Egyptian columns. The Court of Sessions and Tombs Police Court, are held in this building. It also comprises the prison, which has about 150 cells. The place of execution of criminals is in the interior court yard. The edifice was completed in 1838. On application to the Commissioners of Public Charities and Correction, visitors may obtain admission to the prison.

THE DEPARTMENT OF CHARITIES AND CORRECTION

Have erected, on the corner of Eleventh street and Third avenue, a neat and substantial building, which they occupy. This very important department was created by an act of the State Legislature, and is the most benevolent institution in the city. Almost hourly through the winter the rooms are crowded with applicants for relief, whose wants are amply and promptly attended to. A large and very efficient corps of assistants are employed to carry out the objects for which this institution was created. This department is under the management of a Board of Five Commissioners, who have entire control over all the public institutions of the city, including Randall's, Ward's, and Blackwell's Islands. Any persons desirous of visiting any or all of these places can obtain permits at this office.

THE CITY ARMORY.

The old City Armory, or Arsenal, is situated at the junction of Elm and White streets, extending 84 feet on Elm and 131 feet on White street. The edifice is so constructed that, in case of any popular tumult, it could be defended by a garrison of fifty men. The ground floor is used as a gun room, and the upper room for drilling. The style of the architecture is a kind of gothic, with castellated towers. This arsenal contains a portion of the artillery of the first division of the New York State Militia. The new Arsenal is situated on the corner of Thirty-fifth street and Seventh avenue, and is a much larger edifice.

THE CUSTOM HOUSE,

Occupying the building which was formerly the Merchants'

Exchange, is located between Wall street, Exchange Place, William and Hanover streets. The material employed in its construction is blue Quincy granite, and it is characterized by fine proportions and massive substantial appearance. Its dimensions are on such a scale as to produce a fine architectural effect, being in length 200 feet; in width, from 144 to 171; while it has an elevation of 77 feet at the cornice, and 124 at the top of the dome. The portico of eighteen Ionic columns, which graces its front, imparts to it an imposing effect. The interior of the building fully sustains the impression; for, besides the numerous apartments set apart to various uses, it contains a rotunda in the centre, surmounted by a lofty dome, which is supported in part by eight Corinthian columns of Italian marble. This rotunda is capable of containing 3,000 persons. Its entire cost, including the ground, was over $1,800,000. The architect was Isaiah Rogers; and it was built on the site of the old Exchange, destroyed by the fire of 1835. The original stockholders lost every penny of their investment, it having been sold to other hands to defray the mortgage held by the Barings of London.

THE UNITED STATES TREASURY AND ASSAY OFFICE,

On the corner of Wall and Nassau streets is a splendid building, constructed in the Doric order of Grecian architecture. It is built in the most substantial manner, of white marble, something after the model of the Parthenon at Athens: as a piece of masonry, it is equal to any structure extant, and to judge from appearances, likely to become as enduring as the Pyramids; it occupies the site of the old Federal Hall. The building is 200 feet long, 80 feet high: at the southern end, on Wall street is a portico of eight purely Grecian columns, 34 feet in height; and on the northern end, on Pine street, is a corresponding portico of similar columns. The great business hall is a splendid room, 60 feet in diameter. The cost of the building, including the ground, was $1,195,000.

THE OLD POST OFFICE,

In Nassau street, between Cedar and Liberty streets, was formerly the Middle Dutch Church. During the war of the Revolution, when most of the churches were turned to military use by the British, this one sustained the greatest injuries; which more or less, however, fell upon all. In 1790 it received such repairs as fitted it again for public worship; but it was afterwards secured by the government and devoted to its present use. It was in the old wooden steeple of this building that Franklin practiced his experiments in electricity.

THE NEW POST OFFICE,

Now in process of construction, and in fact very nearly completed, on a site situated at the southern end of the City Hall Park, promises to be the finest structure of the kind in the United States.

The style of architecture is the pure French Renaissance. It is three stories high, surmounted by a Mansard roof, marked by a centre pavilion four stories high. The pavilion in front will be 160 feet high, and the building facing the City Hall will be 320 feet in length. The first story will be 22 feet high, composed of arched openings, supported upon square piers; the second will be 18 feet high, and the third 16. The style of the building is that of the Tuilleries and the Hotel de Ville. The building will display the following statues: America, Commerce, Industry, Washington, Franklin, Justice, History, Peace, Strength, Truth, Genius of the Arts, Virtue, Honor, Literature, Mechanics, Genius of Science, Agriculture, and

Navigation. The public corridor is 25 feet wide, and 600 feet in length, entered from Broadway and Park Row. The Building will be completed, it is claimed, during the present winter, though from present appearances it is not likely to be entirely finished under a twelve-month. Clocks are to be placed at various points around the building, for the accommodation of the public.

POST OFFICE REGULATIONS.

Money order Department, Nassau street corner Liberty: office hours, 10 a. m., to 3 p. m. No letter is sent from this office to places within the United States, unless the postage is prepaid *by stamps*. Inland postage upon single letters (half an ounce and under) is three cents, and for every additional half ounce or less, there is an additional charge of one single postage. City letters must also be prepaid (two cents) *by stamps*, for every half ounce. The Mails close as follows:

Philadelphia Mail,		5 a. m., and 4:30 p. m.
Northern	"	5 a. m., 2 and 4 p. m.
Eastern	"	5:30 a. m., 1:30 and 6 p. m.
Southern	"	7 a. m., and 6 p. m.
Western	"	5 a. m., and 4 p. m.

THE GRAND CENTRAL RAILWAY STATION.

This magnificent structure, the largest of its kind, and incomparably the most elegant in the country, the most complete, and the best adapted for its purposes of any in the world, is a noble and fit monument to the foresight of its eminent projector, and is well worth a visit and careful inspection by any stranger.

The building, which has an average height of 60 feet, extends from Forty-second street to Forty-fifth street, 692 feet;

and from Fourth avenue to a new street on the west side, which runs from Forty-second to Forty-fifth street, 240 feet. On three sides the walls are of brick, with iron trimmings. The Forty-fifth street front is cast iron. The roof is wrought iron supported by semi-circular trusses 199 feet span, and has a clear height of 90 feet, covered with galvanized iron, and glass. The building is in the Renaissance style of architecture, and is supplied with every necessary appointment.

The ground floor on the Forty-Second street front is occupied by the New Haven Company, for waiting and baggage rooms; the side on the new street by the Harlem and Hudson River Companies for the same purposes; the trains entering at the Forty-fifth street front. The second story furnishes business offices for the three companies.

Passengers for the trains are admitted by way of the waiting rooms. City horse-cars are admitted to the depot on the arrival of trains, for the accommodation of passengers.

THE PUBLIC MARKETS.

There is little to be seen at any of the markets of the city to interest the stranger. The two principal markets, Washington and Fulton, are a couple of tumble-down shanties, encumbered with every nuisance which it is possible to concentrate around a market. If, however, the visitor should be interested in farm produce, and would like to see such quantities of it as he probably never dreamed of, he is recommended to rise early some Saturday morning and go down to Washington Market. Go all through both the regular and outside markets; then go around the intersecting streets for half a mile each way and count, if he can, the farmers' wagons he will find there, loaded down with produce; then let him calculate the quantity, and imagine where there are people enough to eat it all.

PUBLIC WORKS.

THE CROTON AQUEDUCT,

By which the city is supplied with pure water, is one of the most gigantic enterprises of the kind ever undertaken in any country. The distance which the water travels through this artificial channel, exclusive of the grand reservoir, is about 40 miles. The Dam crosses the Croton River six miles from its mouth, and the whole distance from this dam, thirty-two miles, is one unbroken underground canal, formed of stone and brick. The cost of this immense undertaking was over $13,000,000. The great receiving reservoir is in the Central Park, five miles from the City Hall; it can receive a depth of water to the extent of twenty feet, and is capable of containing 150,000,000 gallons. Two miles further on is the distributing reservoir, at Murray Hill. This one is of solid masonry, built in the Egyptian style of architecture, with massive buttresses and hollow granite walls. On the top of the wall is an enclosed promenade.

During the past few years the works have been thoroughly examined and repaired from the Croton Dam to the receiving reservoir, at an immense cost. In connection with this a topographical survey of the valley of the Croton was effected, by which it appears that the ridge defining the waters above the point at which the Aqueduct begins, measures 101 miles. Within this circuit there are 31 lakes and ponds; and the aggregate area of waters, including the tributaries, is 352 square miles; which is equal to 96,034 gallons per square mile, during the dryest season.

Among the improvements now contemplated in these colossal works, is the erection of still another immense reservoir, in the north-eastern part of the city, provided with a high column of water (pumped up by steam) in order to increase the pressure in the pipes of the division where the present head of water is ineffective, owing to the altitude of the ground.

The great Receiving Reservoir cost $2,250,000, and is located at York Hill, in the Central Park, between Eighty-fifth and Ninety-seventh streets. The gate-houses are built in the outer reservoir bank, and at the ends of the central bank. The south gate-house is located near Eighty-sixth street; 83 feet long, 40 feet wide, and 42 feet above the pavement of the bays, which are to be divided. The masonry is very massive, and supported by buttresses 4 feet wide and 16 feet high. The north gate-house will be 72 feet by 40, and corresponds with the others so far as relates to distribution.

HIGH BRIDGE.

This most important structure, connected with the Croton Aqueduct, is situated at the distance of about eight miles from the City Hall. It is thrown across the Harlem valley and river. It spans the whole width of the valley and river at a point where the latter is 620 feet wide, and the former a quarter of a mile. Eight arches, each with a span of 80 feet, compose this structure; and the elevation of the arches gives 100 feet clear of the river from their lower side. Besides these there are several other arches rising from the ground, the span of which is somewhat more than half that of the first mentioned. The material employed throughout the whole of this imposing object is granite. The works cost $900,000. The water is led over this bridge, which is 1,453 feet in extent, in iron pipes; and over all is a pathway which, though wide enough for carriages, is available to pedestrians only. It can be reached pleasantly and expeditiously by the Harlem Railroad, or in summer by the Third avenue horse cars, and steamboat from Harlem. The sail up the Harlem on the little steamer is a very charming one. The surrounding scenery is fine, and the Bridge is constantly in view.

If we go by water, we shall pass the old-fashioned tavern and grounds of McComb's Dam—once a favorite halting place with the owners of fast teams, but of late given up to the training of prize fighters, *et al.*, and long since cast in the shade by the more opulent and fashionable houses on the other side of the stream. As we proceed up the river, the banks on either side grow more bold and precipitous, and a single turn in our course gives us a full view of High Bridge itself.

On the lofty bank at the lower extremity of the bridge is situated a restaurant, whose saloons are, in pleasant weather, thronged with gentlemen and ladies refreshing themselves after their drives. The grounds in the rear include an orchard and handsome gardens, while verdant lawns slope steeply to the water's edge.

THE EAST RIVER BRIDGE.

This long-needed means of additional facilities of communication with its principal suburb, is now in a fair way of being realized by the City of New York. The new bridge will be of more importance, perhaps, to Brooklyn than to New York, if we regard them as distinct cities; but, in fact, Brooklyn is as much a part of New York as Harlem is. More than 100,000 of its male inhabitants cross over the ferries to New York every day to their business; their bedrooms and business being much nearer together than they would be if they lived above Twentieth street in New York City. The day is probably not far distant when the two cities will be incorporated under one government.

The work on the bridge is progressing rapidly. The abutments on both sides already tower above the surrounding objects. The landing place on the New York side will be in the vicinity of the City Hall Park. The Brooklyn terminus will be in the vicinity of the corner of Sands and Fulton streets. It is not expected that the bridge will be completed under five years.

HARLEM BRIDGE.

The new Harlem Bridge, which is built of iron, is a rather clumsy looking structure, and has cost the counties of New York and Westchester about double what it should have done; but it is certainly an immense improvement over the rickety old wooden affair which it superseded. Just above it is the railroad bridge, over which almost constantly trundle the trains of the Harlem River and New Haven Railroads.

At this point and vicinity, both above and below the bridges, a large number of boats and little smacks are constantly moored in the fishing season, and a pleasant row on the smooth bosom of the delightful little river may be enjoyed at a small expense. These, with the expansive water view looking toward the mouth of the stream, with the salt, seaweedy smell of the tides as they wash through the long grasses of the flats, serve to render the place picturesque and agreeable, and thousands seek the vicinity, by boat and rail, on holidays and summer Sundays.

BENEVOLENT INSTITUTIONS.

The traveler who comes to the city by way of the East River will not fail to notice the elegant and extensive public buildings on Ward's, Randall's, and Blackwell's Islands, opposite the upper end of the island. These are all city institutions, such as Alms-houses, Hospitals, Nurseries, Penitentiary, Idiot Asylum, Insane Asylum, Inebriate Asylum, Prisons, etc., etc.

They are all under the direction of the Department of Charities and Correction. Office, **N. W.** corner of Third avenue and 11th street.

Any stranger who may wish to visit either or all of these institutions, must call at the office of the Department, where he can obtain a pass, and learn on what day, and how, he can reach the particular institution.

BLACKWELL'S ISLAND.

A visit to the several establishments on this island will well repay any one interested in the efforts for ameliorating human suffering. There are on the island the Penitentiary, with its 500 to 1,000 convicts, the Alms-house, Hospital, the Lunatic Asylum, and the New Work-house—which last is one of the most complete edifices in the country. It is built of stone taken from the quarries of the island. It is a very spacious building, being capable of holding about 600 persons; all its internal arrangements are very complete. The humane object of this institution is to separate vagrants from criminals, and to compel all to work who are able to do something towards their own support. The building, which is 325 feet in length, cost about $100,000. There are various modes of conveyance thither,— by the Second or Third avenue cars, and by steamer which leaves foot of Twenty-seventh street, East River.

RANDALL'S ISLAND.

Here are the nurseries for the support and instruction of destitute children. This institution is the most interesting of all, and commends itself to the sympathies of all who would become acquainted with the benevolent agencies of New York city. There are usually to be seen here, in the several institutions, from 4,000 to 5,000 persons young and old.

THE BLOOMINGDALE ASYLUM FOR THE INSANE,

Is situated on the Bloomingdale Road, at a distance of about seven miles from the City Hall. It occupies a most beautiful and commanding site, and its approach and surroundings are admirably fitted to lighten the sense of depression and gloom which we instinctively associate with every establishment of the kind. The treatment administered to its unfortunate inmates, too, is of the most enlightened, humane and rational sort. The principal building is 211 feet in length, 60 in depth, and four stories in height, with side buildings.

The approach to the Asylum from the southern entrance, by the stranger who generally associates the most sombre scenes with a lunatic hospital, is highly pleasing. The sudden opening of the view, the extent of the grounds, the various avenues gracefully winding through so large a lawn, the cedar hedges, the fir and other ornamental trees tastefully distributed or grouped, and the variety of shrubbery and flowers, presents a charming picture not often to be found in connection with institutions of this nature.

The central building is always open to visitors; and the view from the top of it, being the most extensive and beautiful of any in the vicinity of the city, is well worthy of their attention.

THE NEW YORK JUVENILE ASYLUM,

A stone edifice, situated near High Bridge, is a home and reformatory for neglected children. The asylum by its charter becomes the legal guardian of all such children as may be committed to it by the voluntary act of their parents or by the precept of a police magistrate. The institution owes its origin to Dr. J. E. Russ of this city, so favorably known for his exertions in establishing the New York Institution for the Blind. The success of the institution has been largely promoted by A. R. Wetmore, Esq., who has been its president and financier almost from its organization. It occupies about 20 acres of ground, which is in part cultivated by the children who, during their stay in the asylum, are instructed in all the branches of a common school education. As soon as their improvement will warrant their removal they are sent to the Great West and indentured, where, in a few years, instead of being drawn into the vortex of crime as they almost inevitably would have been, if left unprotected in our streets, they will many of them become our law-makers and occupy places of trust. The institution has a house of reception for 200 children, in West Thirteenth street. All children when first committed must remain in this house ten days to afford their parents an opportunity of reclaiming them. The two buildings can accommodate about 700. Take Hudson River railroad or Manhattanville stages to Fort Washington or High Bridge.

THE NEW YORK ORPHAN ASYLUM,

Situated in Bloomingdale near Eightieth street, comprises a fine building 120 feet by 60, and nine acres of ground laid out with much taste. These grounds command a splendid view of the Hudson and East Rivers, with the surrounding scenery. There are in this institution about 200 orphans. The institution was incorporated by charter in 1807, and its present edifice was completed in 1840. It is a most praiseworthy institution, and a very interesting one to visit.

THE MAGDALENE ASYLUM,

Situate west of the Harlem Railroad, on Eighty-eighth street, near Fifth avenue. This praiseworthy institution, as its name indicates, has been established for the recovery and restoration of fallen and distressed females. It is well sustained; and by the self-sacrificing labors of the benevolent, has been productive of great good.

THE ASYLUM FOR AGED INDIGENT FEMALES

Is located in Twentieth street, near Second avenue. Its title indicates sufficiently the object of the institution, which is both well filled and well sustained.

THE INSTITUTION FOR THE BLIND

Is on Ninth avenue, between Thirty-third and Thirty-fourth streets, occupying thirty-two lots of ground presented by James Boorman, Esq. The edifice is of granite and of the Gothic order of architecture. It owes it origin mainly to Dr. J. D. Russ, whose attention was directed to the sightless condition of a large number of the children in the City Alms-house. Moved by the spectacle he determined to devote himself to their relief, and for that purpose took seven children from the Alms-house and gratuitously instructed them for nearly two years, and finally obtained the passage of an Act by the Legislature for their support. In this effort he was ably supported by Samuel Wood, a well known member of the Society of Friends, and Dr. Samuel

Akerly, distinguished for his zeal and labors in behalf of the Institution for the deaf and dumb. Here also the usual branches of education are taught, and the pupils are instructed in the several useful arts of life. It is an exceedingly useful object to visit, as is also the Deaf and Dumb Asylum. The institution is open to visitors on week days from 1 to 6 p. m., and may be conveniently reached by the Eighth or Ninth avenue railroads.

THE INSTITUTION FOR THE DEAF AND DUMB.

This noble and well-conducted asylum is situated at Fanwood, Washington Heights, on 162d street, which is reached by means of the Hudson River railroad. The principal building measures 110 feet by 60, and is five stories high. It is capable of accommodating from 200 to 300 pupils, exclusive of the principals and teachers, etc. It is one of the best-endowed institutions of benevolence in New York, being sustained by appropriations made by the State Legislature, by the City Corporation, and private benefactions. The pupils are instructed in the ordinary branches of learning, and some of them in the various trades. Open to the public from half-past 1 to 4 p. m., every day.

THE HOUSE OF INDUSTRY,

In the Five Points, near Centre and Pearl streets. Placed in the very midst of squalid poverty and crime, this excellent charity has achieved great results in rescuing and reclaiming the youth of vicious parentage. Mr. Pease's institution dates back only to 1848, yet thus far has its progress been incomparably the most successful of any of the numerous noble charities of New York. Persevering through numberless difficulties Mr. Pease at length has achieved a great success in his laudable endeavors. He has now from 100 to 200 inmates, rescued from the purlieus of vice and poverty, hopefully engaged in his House of Industry. Since its foundation several hundred women have been sent out to places in the country. By his economical plan, the major part of the expenses of the establishment have been defrayed by the productive labor of the inmates.

THE HOUSE OF INDUSTRY AND HOME FOR THE FRIENDLESS

Is located on Thirtieth street, between Fourth and Madison avenues. It is under the direction of a society devoted to the protection of deserted children, and adult persons who may be in distress. This association has largely contributed to the relief of the poor and destitute of the city,—in one year it relieved and provided with places over 600 young and old. The society publishes a paper semi-monthly, entitled *The Advocate and Guardian,* which has a circulation of about 15,000 copies; it has also published over 10,000 tracts, etc.

THE LEAKE AND WATTS ORPHAN HOUSE

Was founded in 1827, by a legacy of Mr. J. G. Leake. It is located on the block bounded by Ninth and Tenth avenues and 111th and 112th streets. The income of the institution is able to support two or three hundred orphans.

THE SOCIETY FOR THE RELIEF OF POOR WIDOWS WITH SMALL CHILDREN,

Was organized in 1797, by the efforts of the late Mrs. Isabella Graham. Its average number of persons relieved annualy is about 200 widows and 500 children.

THE NEW YORK DISPENSARIES.

These are associations for giving medicine and medical advice to the poor. The Northern Dispensary, situated on the corner of Christopher and Sixth streets, was founded in 1829; and the Eastern Dispensary, on the corner of Ludlow street and Essex Market Place, was instituted in 1834. There is also a still older Dispensary, on the corner of White and Centre streets, established in 1795; and is estimated to have given relief to more than 100,000 patients since its first organization.

THE DEMILT DISPENSARY

Is a fine building at the corner of the Second avenue and Twenty-third street which, with the ground, cost $30,000—the noble donation of the late Miss Demilt. About 3,000 patients are annually benefited by this noble charity of a single benefactor.

THE BELLEVUE HOSPITAL,

Under the management of the Board of Commissioners of Charities and Correction, is located at Twenty-sixth street and East River. The accommodations here are also excellent.

ST. LUKE'S HOSPITAL,

At the corner of Fifth avenue and Fifty-fourth street, is an admirable charity institution, sustained by members of the Episcopal Churches of New York.

THE SAILORS' SNUG HARBOR,

An asylum for aged and infirm seamen, is situated on the north side of Staten Island. It was founded by Captain Randall in 1801, and incorporated in 1806 in New York: the present noble building on Staten Island, measures 225 feet in length, with 160 acres of ground; about 300 aged and disabled seamen are here supported. Near the Quarantine grounds are the Seamen's Retreat for the sick, and the Home for Sailor's Children; also, the Marine Hospital, which is supported by an emigrant tax of $2 on every cabin passenger native of a foreign country, and 50 cents for every steerage passenger. The fund from these sources, amounts to nearly $100,000 per annum.

SOCIETIES AND ASSOCIATIONS.

YOUNG MEN'S CHRISTIAN ASSOCIATION OF THE CITY OF NEW YORK.

This association was organized June, 1852, for "the improvement of the spiritual, mental, social and physical condition of young men." It was designed more particularly for young men from the country, who came to the great city to enter into business. These young men are often crowded into uncomfortable boarding-houses, with little to make the evenings pass profitably or pleasantly, and easily become a prey to those who are ever on the alert to lead young men into evil. The association carried on its work quietly, but successfully, in obscure rooms until December, 1869, when they took possession of their spacious building on the corner of Twenty-third street and Fourth avenue.

The style of the building is French Renaissance, and it is faced with freestone in two colors, the general ground being of Belleville stone of a rich purple hue, and the mouldings and cornices being of buff-colored Ohio freestone—a color nearly complimentary to the former.

THE COOPER UNION

Is a noble building erected by Mr. Peter Cooper, of New York, and is devoted to the "moral, intellectual, and physical improvement of his countrymen." The building covers an entire block on Third avenue, Fourth avenue, Seventh and Eighth streets. It is in the immediate vicinity of the new Bible House, the Astor Library, the Mercantile Library, and the rooms of various literary and scientific societies. In the basement is a large lecture-room; and this, and also the first and second stories, which are arranged for stores and offices, are rented so as to provide a revenue to meet the annual expenses of the institute. The institute proper, or the "Union," commences with the second story, in which are the reading rooms and library. On the third and fourth stories are located the schools of science and art. The cost of the building has been $630,000, and the annual income from the rented parts is from $50,000 to $60,000. The whole is under the control of a board of trustees for the benefit of the public; the course of lectures, the library, and the reading rooms are all free. In the munificence both of the gift and the endowment, the Cooper Institute stands as a monument to its noble-hearted founder more enduring than the pyramids. The School of Design, for women, has rooms in this building. Term, from October to June with accommodation for about 150 students. Here also may be found Dr. Colton's establishment for the administering of nitrous-oxide or laughing gas, and the extraction of teeth under its influence. This, one of the most marvelous discoveries of modern times, was the original idea of Dr. Wells, of Boston, a noted dentist, but to Dr. Colton is due the honor of having been the first to put the discovery to a practical use. Since 1863, when he first established himself here, he has administered the gas to some seventy thousand patients, and that, without experiencing a single accident.

INDEPENDENT ORDER OF ODD FELLOWS.

The Independent Order of Odd Fellows number in New York city about 90 lodges, and about 12 encampments, including thousands of members; many of the lodges have fine halls in various parts of this city and the neighboring cities of Brooklyn, Williamsburgh, Jersey City, etc.; but the grand rendezvous of the order is the large brown stone building at the corner of Grand and Centre streets, erected at a cost of $125,000. This imposing edifice presents a noble appearance, being substantially built, lofty and surmounted by a dome. It contains a series of highly ornamented lodge-rooms, richly furnished and in different styles of architecture, some Egyptian, Grecian, Elizabethan, etc. These elegant apartments are well worthy a visit. The average receipts of the association which owns this edifice is about $75,000 annually. Their distribution in the form of benefactions to the sick and poor is on a scale of corresponding liberality.

THE AMERICAN ETHNOLOGICAL SOCIETY,

Founded in 1842. The first President of this Society was the late Albert Gallatin, formerly Secretary of the Treasury, etc., who held the office until his death in 1846. The object of the Society is "the prosecution of inquiries into the origin, progress and characteristics of the various races of men." This Society has collected a large amount of materials, and has published three volumes of Transactions.

THE AMERICAN BIBLE SOCIETY BUILDING,

Which is approached from Broadway through Astor Place, occupies three-fourths of an acre of ground, bounded by Third and Fourth avenues, and Eighth and Ninth streets. The form of this gigantic edifice is nearly triangular. It is the property of the American Bible Society. This imposing looking edifice, which is substantially built of brick, with stone facings, cost nearly $300,000. The principal entrance, which is on the Fourth avenue, has four columns surmounted by a cornice. In the fourth story is a stone figure representing Religion holding a Bible.

The receipts of the Society, at the first year of its

organization in 1816–17, were $37,779,035; its receipts since then amount to about $5,000,000. It has put in circulation about nine millions of Bibles and Testaments, and given some $500,000 to various missionary stations to aid in the publication of the Holy Scriptures. It has supplied thousands of seamen and criminals with copies, as well as distributed hundreds of thousands to private families, hotels, etc., in every part of the United States. It has produced editions of the Bible, or portions of it, in about twenty-four different dialects, and aided in issuing it in others.

THE NEW YORK HISTORICAL SOCIETY,

Established upwards of half a century, have a noble edifice on the corner of Eleventh street and Second avenue. It is an elegant fire-proof structure, built of yellow sandstone from the province of New Brunswick, and is splendidly fitted up. Its literary collections consist of rare and valuable books pertaining to the history and antiquities of the country; also medals, coins, maps, engravings, etc. The library comprises about 20,000 volumes. There is a fine picture gallery in the uppermost story; the library hall, lecture room, and various offices are characterized by great architectural beauty. Recently there have been added a fine collection of Nineveh marbles, presented by James Lenox, Esq., and Dr. Abbott's Egyptian collection (obtained by liberal subscription), one of the most valuable museums of Egyptian antiquities in the world. It contains several hundred relics collected with great care and industry by the learned Dr. Abbott, during a residence of twenty years on the banks of the Nile. Here are to be seen mummied men and quadrupeds, the slates of the school-boys in Pharaoh's time, and the remains of the lamps that were used to lighten the darkness of Egypt. Many of the objects here are three thousand years old.

THE NATIONAL ACADEMY OF DESIGN.

The new building for the National Academy of Design, on the corner of Twenty-third street and Fourth avenue, is one of the most remarkable structures in the city. Principally so, because it is the most prominent example thus far set before the public of the effort now being made to revive the Gothic architecture of the thirteenth century in its true spirit, and adapt it to our own circumstances, materials, and necessities. The public have, unfortunately, been led to call it Venetian Gothic; and, from its similarity in proportion and the fact that the upper story is decorated with diagonal lines of color introduced into the wall itself, and has no windows, to suppose that it is a copy of the famous Ducal Palace. But a careful examination, in comparison with a good photograph of that building, will dispel the delusion.

The carvings on the capitals of the first and second stories are well worthy of careful examination, and are more particularly remarkable from the fact that they are almost entirely designed by the men who carved them, and are the result of careful study from natural leaves and flowers. The work of the architect, in connection with this decorative work, consisted principally of instructions given to the workmen in the art of design applied to their own work.

The fronts of the buildings are built of white Winchester county marble, banded with gray-wacke. The ornamented iron work of the exterior is worthy of careful attention, being entirely wrought out on the anvil. The main entrance-gates are wonderful for their lightness, careful finish, and strength, being the most elaborate piece of architectural wrought iron in this country.

The building is very handsomely finished throughout with white pine, ash, mahogany, oak, and black walnut;

no paint being used, but all the woods showing their natural grain.

The grand staircase approaching the galleries is of solid oak, trimmed with walnut, finished in wood on the under as well as upper sides.

The annual exhibitions of the Academy are held during the months of April, May, June, and July, during which time the building is open to the public for a small admission fee. The works of living artists only are exhibited, and no pictures are accepted that have been previously exhibited in New York.

The exhibition of the Artists' Fund Society is generally held in the galleries of the Academy, and takes place in November and December annually. It is a noble charity, devoted to the relief of sick and poor artists.

THE LYCEUM OF NATURAL HISTORY

Is a society of scientific men, formed for the study of natural history. Its rooms are in Fourteenth street, near the Fourth avenue. It possesses a good library, and a large museum of minerals, plants, and specimens of natural history. It is accessible to the public.

THE METROPOLITAN MUSEUM OF ART,

For which an imposing edifice is now being erected in the Central Park, on the Fifth avenue, between Eightieth and Eighty-fourth streets, is now temporarily located in East Fourteenth street, between Sixth and Seventh avenues, in the old Douglas mansion. Here are to be seen a fine collection of paintings by the "old masters," statuary, porcelain, arms and armor, coins, engravings, and old books, well worthy of the attention of those who take an interest in these matters. The celebrated Cissnola collection of statuary, pottery, bronze instruments, jewels, etc., excavated some years since in the island of Cyprus, from the site of the old Phœnecian cities that existed some centuries before the birth of Christ, is now the property of the Museum, having been purchased of the discoverer for the sum of $60,000, and is now on exhibition here. Admission on Mondays is free, on other days a small fee is exacted.

THE NATIONAL RIFLE ASSOCIATION.

Although the introduction of the rifle as a military weapon was owing to the lessons of our Revolution, and although our success in the earlier contests of our history depended upon the skill in its use displayed by our ancestors, no recognition has been given by our citizens of the fact that the change which has taken place in the habits of the American people is rapidly depriving them of that personal skill in arms and marksmanship which has hitherto formed one of the greatest elements of our national strength. Other nations have long since instituted a thorough system of instruction in rifle practice. France, Germany, Switzerland, and, above all, England and Canada, unite in giving to rifle practice a leading position in their systems of military training. In the latter countries the success that has been attained, not only in producing good marksmen, but in making the subject popular among the people at large, has been very great.

In this country, on the other hand, the matter has been entirely neglected, although our entire system of defense is based upon the levying of volunteers in cases of emergency, who, to be valuable, or even available, must understand the use of arms, and supply by their skill as individuals the confidence which discipline gives to regular troops.

This anomalous condition of affairs having excited considerable discussion among military men through the press, finally, on November 24, 1871, led to the formation in the

City of New York of The National Rifle Association, which was designed, and bids fair to be the parent of many similar associations throughout the country.

The Association is organized under the general act in in regard to clubs, which exempts the members from personal liability, but makes the directors liable for all debts not contracted on a credit of over a year.

The annual dues of members are $3; the payment of $25 constituting a life membership, free from all other dues or assessments.

Rifle associations or military organizations (outside the limits of the first and second division districts of the National Guard), by paying not less than $25 are entitled to a membership for every $1.50 paid, and to have the reports of their matches published in the annual report of the Association.

The work of selecting grounds of a sufficient extent for a range which should be at once cheap, safe, and convenient of access, proved no easy task. Finally a purchase was made of a tract of seventy acres, situated upon the Central Railroad of Long Island, twelve miles from Hunter's Point, and within half an hour's ride of Thirty-fourth street ferry in New York City.

These grounds are admirably adapted for the purpose for which they have been selected. As level as a billiard table, they afford twenty separate ranges, each of which can be used from one hundred to a thousand yards, and without the use of elevated firing stands, found necessary upon most English and Canadian ranges. In addition, ample room is left for "pool" targets, and a "running man," as well as for camp purposes and distance drill.

LIBRARIES.

THE ASTOR LIBRARY,

Lafayette Place, one block east of Broadway, owes its existence to the noble bequest of its founder, John Jacob Astor, Esq., who, in a codicil to his will, appropriated the sum of $400,000 for its establishment and maintenance. According to the provisions of the bequest, $75,000 was the sum authorized to be applied for the erection of the building; $120,000 for the purchase of books; and the residue of the $400,000 to be invested in real estate on bond or mortgages, the interest of which is to be applied to defray the expenses of maintaining the Library.

The entire collection of books amounts to 140,000 volumes. The whole value of the estate is about $1,250,000. The real value of the collection is not to be estimated by its numerical extent or its pecuniary cost, but by its intrinsic value of its books. In this respect the Astor Library takes precedence of all others in this country. It is frequented by a class of readers principally composed of students and professional men, but it is also free to all, without exception, who desire to consult the rare and valuable works to be found in its alcoves, in every department of science and literature. The Library continues steadily to increase. Particular attention is paid to technology; American history is very full, and in linguistic works it is unsurpassed by any in the country. Natural science is fully represented, and, in short, in magnificent provision for the intellectual development of the great public it is doubtful whether it is second to any on the continent. During the past few months there have been extensive additions to the Library. Rare and valuable classical works, works on history, travel, archaeology, and recent publications in French, English, and Latin have been purchased. The accessions to the scientific department, consisting of mathematics, astronomy, mechanics, agriculture, engineering, botany, and architecture, have been selected with much discrimination; and the departments embracing works of reference in medicine, geology, natural history, theology, chemistry, etc., are now valuably supplied. There is also a large collection of magazines, bound newspapers (foreign and domestic), maps, charts, ancient illuminated books, historical annuals, and American and European official documents going back to remote dates, which show the variety of sources which have been drawn upon by the trustees since the establishment of the Library.

THE SOCIETY LIBRARY

Is located at 67 University Place, east side, between Twelfth and Thirteenth streets. It is, perhaps, the oldest public library in the United States. It was incorporated in the year 1700 under the name of "The Public Library of New York." In 1754 its corporate name was changed to "The New York Society Library." The building, which belongs to the Society, is about 50 feet front, very plain and unpretentious, but being designed for the library is well adapted to its purpose. The number of volumes in this library is about 45,000; some of them are very rare. The library is open week days, from 8 A. M. till sunset, and the reading rooms until 10 P. M. Twenty-five dollars is the fee for membership, and six dollars per annum the dues.

MERCANTILE LIBRARY

Occupies the Clinton Hall building in Astor Place, Eighth street. This noble establishment comprises a fine library, and reading room. Its literary collections number upwards of 150,000 volumes, in the several departments of general knowledge, including also a valuable series of 500 periodical works, unsurpassed by any other institution. The number of books circulated each year is about 275,000. The number of its members at the present time exceeds 10,000. This institution, originally established for the use of clerks, has been since thrown open to the public on payment of the subscription, $5 per annum.

THE APPRENTICES' LIBRARY,

Containing about 50,000 volumes, for the use of youthful apprentices, is in the Mechanics' Hall, 472 Broadway, near Grand street.

COLLEGES AND SEMINARIES.

THE COLLEGE OF THE CITY OF NEW YORK,

In Twenty-third street, corner of Lexington avenue, was established in 1848, by the Board of Education of the City of New York, in pursuance of an act passed May 7, 1847, for the purpose of providing higher education for such pupils of the common schools as may wish to avail themselves thereof. The college is under the general superintendence of the Board of Education; but it is specially under the supervision of an Executive Committee, for its care, government, and management, appointed by the Board. All its expenses for instruction, apparatus, library, cabinet, collections, books, and stationery, are paid out of the public treasury.

The students are admitted in annual classes, and the full course of study embraces five years.

The Board of Education is authorized by law to confer for the usual collegiate degrees on the recommendation of the faculty.

Graduates may become "Resident Graduates," and continue their studies at option. The academical studies during term time, continue daily (except Saturday and Sunday).

THE NEW YORK UNIVERSITY

Is located on the east side of Washington Square, and forms a noble architectural ornament, being of the English collegiate style of architecture. The University was established in 1831, and has ever maintained its high reputation. It has a chancellor, and a corps of professors in the various departments of learning. There is also a grammar school connected with the institution; also, a valuable library, philosophical apparatus, etc. The edifice is of marble, and presents a very beautiful appearance as seen through the thick foliage of the park. The great central gothic window lights the chapel of the University; divine service is held here every Sunday at the usual hours. The principal entrance is by the centre door, up a flight of marble steps. In the upper parts of the building are several chambers and offices occupied by various societies, literary persons and artists.

COLUMBIA COLLEGE,

Originally chartered by George II, in 1754, under the title of King's College, till within a short period stood in Park Place. In 1784 its name was changed to Columbia

College. Alexander Hamilton, John Randolph of Roanoke, De Witt Clinton, and many others of the leading men of this country have been among its graduates. In 1857 the college was removed to its present site, on Forty-ninth street, near the Fifth avenue. It has a president and twelve professors; a choice library of rare classical works, of about 18,000 volumes, museum, etc. A grammar school is attached to the institution, over which a professor presides as rector.

COLLEGE OF ST. FRANCIS XAVIER.

This institution, situated on Fifteenth street, between Fifth and Sixth avenues, was founded in 1850. With its grammar school it contains about four hundred pupils. The library contains about 25,000 volumes.

MANHATTAN COLLEGE.

This newly incorporated university is situated at Manhattanville.

THE UNION THEOLOGICAL SEMINARY

Is situated No. 9 University Place, between Waverly Place and Eighth street. The principal edifice comprises four large lecture rooms, chapel, and library of 16,000 volumes; also, studies and other rooms for students. It has six professors, and usually about one hundred students. It was founded 1836.

THE GENERAL THEOLOGICAL SEMINARY

Of the Episcopal Church is situated in Twentieth street, corner of Ninth avenue, near the Hudson, two miles from the City Hall. There are two handsome buildings of stone, for the accommodation of professors and students. The Board of Trustees consists of all the bishops, and one trustee from each diocese in the United States. The institution is well endowed and in a flourishing condition.

COLLEGE OF PHYSICIANS AND SURGEONS.

This is a handsome edifice, corner of Twenty-third street and Fourth avenue. It was founded in 1807, has eight professors and about two hundred students. There is a small library here of about 1,500 volumes, and an anatomical museum, accessible to the public.

NEW YORK MEDICAL COLLEGE,

Is located at No. 90 East Thirteenth street. It was chartered in 1850, and is devoted to the instruction of young medical practitioners. It possesses a valuable anatomical museum, chemical laboratory, etc. There is also in this building the College of Pharmacy.

UNIVERSITY MEDICAL COLLEGE

Is connected with the New York University, but is located at the Bellevue Hospital, at the foot of East Twenty-sixth street. It ranks among the highest medical schools, and graduates a large class every year.

THE NEW YORK MEDICAL COLLEGE AND HOSPITAL FOR WOMEN

Is located at 187 Second avenue, and graduates a class of female physicians every year.

CHURCHES.

It is estimated that there are very nearly four hundred churches in New York City; many of them being of great elegance. We annex brief notices of the more prominent and noteworthy.

TRINITY CHURCH.

Fronting Wall street, with its portal invitingly open every day in the year, stands Trinity Chuch, a beautiful temple of worship, in strange contiguity with the busy marts where "merchants most do congregate." It is the third edifice of the kind erected upon the spot, the first having been destroyed in the great fire of 1776. The second, completed in 1790, stood until 1839, when it was taken down and the present fine gothic structure was commenced. It was seven years in building, under the careful superintendence of Mr. Upjohn, the architect. The church is 192 feet in length, 80 in breadth, and 60 in height. The interior will richly repay examination. Among many relics there carefully preserved is an elaborate chancel service of silver, presented to the corporation by Queen Anne.

The steeple towers up 284 feet in height; the walls of the church are nearly 50 feet high, and the whole edifice, both as to its exterior and interior, is regarded by most persons as the most elegant and cathedral-like of the churches in the city.

The graveyard of Old Trinity occupies nearly an entire block. Within it are the venerated tombs of Alexander

Hamilton, the statesman and friend of Washington; the heroic commander Lawrence, and many other illustrious public men.

Adjoining Trinity buildings, and a few feet from Broadway, stands the monumental tribute of the Corporation of Trinity Church to the honored "Sugar House Martyrs." Of finely cut and ornamented brown stone, it presents a graceful appearance, while it attracts the especial interest of every American patriot from the fact that the ground immediately under and around it, is rich with the ashes of our Revolutionary fathers.

No traveler who desires to see the city should leave it without ascending Trinity Church steeple. In a clear day almost every object within a distance of from five to ten miles from the city is distinguishable.

ST. PAUL'S CHAPEL,

The third Episcopal church established in the city, was erected in 1766. It stands between Fulton and Vesey streets.

On the front, in a niche of red sandstone, in the centre of a large pediment, supported by four Ionic columns, is a white marble statue of St. Paul, leaning on a sword. Also in the front part of the niche there is inserted a slab of white marble, bearing an inscription to the memory of General Montgomery, who fell at Quebec during the Revolution, and whose remains were removed to New York by order of the State, in 1818. At the lower side of the church, facing Broadway, is an obelisk of white marble, erected in honor of Thomas Addis Emmet, the Irish patriot and barrister, who died here in 1827.

ST. JOHN'S CHAPEL.

This is one of the associate churches of the Trinity Corporation. It is located opposite the Hudson River

R. R. Freight Depot. It is not modern in style, but yet a very noble looking edifice. It is built of sandstone, and is very spacious.

In all the ancient churches of New York City, the plan of a collegiate charge was the rule. The ancient Episcopal Church of the city was established on this basis. Trinity Church was considered the parish church, and had a collegiate charge; St. George's, St. John's, and St. Paul's were called "Chapels." St. George's is now a distinct charge, but the other two are still collegiate.

GRACE CHURCH

(Episcopal). This superb edifice, the most ornate of the ecclesiastical buildings of New York, is located on Broadway, near Tenth street, and commands a fine view of the great avenue of the city, north and south. The loft spiral and richly decorated steeple is an object of universal admiration. There is one large and two less sized doors in front. Over the main entrance is a circular window of stained glass, and two tall, oblong, windows in each side of the upper section of the tower. Within is a grand array of pillars, carved work, and upwards of forty windows of stained glass, each giving different hues of vision. There is a little too much of theatrical glitter in the interior, to comport with the chastened solemnities of religious worship. It was built in 1845.

ST. GEORGE'S CHURCH

(Episcopal). This spacious and elegant structure, the most capacious ecclesiastical edifice in the city, is situated in East Sixteenth street, opposite Stuyvesant Square. It was erected in 1849, and for architectural beauty is entitled to the first stand among religious edifices of New York. Its imposing exterior and vast interior, unsupported by any visible columns, either to roof or gallery, impart to it a fine effect. Its architecture is of the Byzantine order. The ground upon which the church stands was given by the late Peter G. Stuyvesant. The interior of this splendid church was entirely destroyed by fire, supposed to be the work of an incendiary, during the latter part of 1865, entailing a heavy loss on the society, as it was but partially insured. The fine towers of red sandstone were, however, left intact and uninjured, as were also the massive walls of the building. The interior was accordingly rebuilt, and the edifice now surpasses, in its internal appointments, even its former elegance.

ST. MARK'S CHURCH

(Episcopal), situate in Stuyvesant street, to the east of the Bowery, was built in its present form in 1826.

The steeple is lofty, but somewhat venerable in appearance, which is indeed the character of the entire structure. The church is venerable also on account of its historic associations; it stands on what was the estate of Petrus Stuyvesant, the last of the Dutch governors, and his remains rest in a vault under the church, over which, on the east side, is a tablet indicating the fact. Here also repose the mortal remains of the English governor, Col. Sloughter, and those of the American governor, Tompkins.

THE CHURCH OF THE TRANSFIGURATION

Is situated on the north side of Twenty-ninth street, just east of Fifth avenue, and with its adjoining Chapel and Rectory, more interesting from its quaint irregularity and air of seclusion than for any architectural pretensions. Indeed it may be said to have no architecture at all. The original edifice was erected about twenty-five years ago, with the Rev. G. H. Houghton as Rector and a congregation of three members. From time to time, as the congregation increased in numbers and wealth, additions were made, by appending a little chapel at this end, a porch at that end, and a wing at the side, until finally the the original building itself disappeared, and gave place to another equally quaint and plain. A glimmer of the Gothic seems to pervade the low, simple eaves, with here and there, in a short, slender column or two, perhaps a shadow of the Arabesque, or something else; so that it is in vain to place the whole structure within the confines of any specific order of art.

With its attendant buildings, the church occupies about ten lots on the street; and with the row of small trees in front, and the little green between the buildings, and the iron railing enclosing them, it would seem, were it not for the out-door life and bustle of the near avenue, much like one might imagine that little church wherein Tom Pinch was wont to play the organ near the residence of the architectural Pecksniff.

The size of the interior, however, is far greater than one would suppose. When the chapel is given into the main body of the church, as is the custom, by means of folding-doors, this, with the interior of the wing, stretching southward to the street, affords accommodation for a much larger congregation than those of many buildings of far more pretentious exterior. The ceiling is very low, and of smooth, simple-arched oaken wood—the material of all the furniture. The chancel is comparatively small, and contains, besides the altar, a font of simple and exquisite design, and of the pure Parian. The windows are small and narrow, and prettily stained, as are also the windows over the chancel recess.

The church has recently obtained a world-wide appellation as "The Little Church around the Corner," a term given to it by a neighboring clergyman, who, refusing to bury an actor from his own church, referred the applicants to this one.

THE NEW ST. PATRICK'S CATHEDRAL

Is a vast edifice in the course of construction, between Fifty-first and Fifty-second streets, on the east side of Fifth avenue, which, when completed, will be by far the most magnificent building in the New World.

The structure under consideration was projected by the late Archbishop Hughes, who laid the corner-stone in 1858, during which and the following year the foundations were laid, and a portion of the superstructure built, when work was temporarily suspended. Upon the accession of Archbishop McCloskey, however, a new impetus was given to the work, which has been vigorously prosecuted ever since

The ground occupied (extreme length, 332 feet; general breadth, 132 feet, with an extreme breadth at the transepts of 174 feet) is the most elevated on Fifth avenue, there being a gradual descent both toward the south and toward Central Park on the north. The site, indeed, is singularly happy and fortunate for so great and imposing a structure.

A stratum of solid rock supports the foundations. The first base-course is of Maine granite—the same as was used in the Treasury Building at the national capitol, and the upper surface of the foundations, upon which it rests, are chisel-dressed, and apparently as solid as the crust of the earth.

The material above the base-course is of white marble, from the quarries of Pleasantville, Westchester County—a highly crystalline stone, productive of very beautiful effects, especially in columns and elaborations of the work.

The style of the building is decorated Gothic—that

which prevailed in Europe from the beginning of the thirteenth century to the close of the fourteenth—and will constitute a judicious mean between the heaviness of the latter period and the over-elaboration of later times. Judging from the picture of the building as complete, it appears to be more nearly modelled upon the celebrated Cathedral of Cologne; but there are also fine and correct examples of the same order of architecture in Rheims and Amiens.

The decoration of the front (Fifth avenue) will be unsurpassed by any in this or any other country. There will be a tower and spire on each corner, each measuring 328 feet from the ground to the summit of the cross, and each 32 feet square at the base, and thence to the point at which the form assumes the octagonal—a height of 136 feet. The towers maintain the square form to this height, then rise in octagonal lanterns, 54 feet in height, and then spring into magnificent spires to a further elevation of 138 feet. The towers and spires are to be ornamented with buttresses, niches with statues, and pinnacles so arranged as to disguise the change from the square to the octagon.

The central gable, between the two towers, will be 156 feet high. The main entrance will be richly decorated, flanked on either side by a large painted window, and embowered in carved symbols of religion. It is intended to have this structure completed within ten years.

THE UNITARIAN CHURCH OF THE MESSIAH,

Occupying a commanding site at the northwest corner of Thirty-fourth street and Park avenue, exhibits in its completion many traits of simple beauty. The architecture may be best expressed as the Rhenish-Gothic style. It is built of brick, with gray sandstone trimmings, and covers a space, including a chapel, of 80x145 feet. The entrance on Thirty-fourth street, is of light-colored stone, elaborately carved, and is conceded to be a little gem as a piece of architecture.

The walls of the interior, which are of plain plaster at present, will be decorated and painted at some future day; and the ceiling is of the simple pendant order.

CHURCH OF ALL SOULS

(Unitarian), corner of Fourth avenue and Twentieth street is an eccentric and remarkable edifice, being built in the style of the Italian churches of the middle ages, of brick and delicate cream colored stone in alternate courses. Adjoining the church, on Twentieth street, is the parsonage. Included in the design is a spire or campanile 300 feet high, but there appears to be no likelihood of its ever being erected.

THE DUTCH REFORMED CHURCH,

Situated on Fourth street and Lafayette Place, was built in 1839. Its interior is characterized by simple elegance. The pulpit is of white marble. The Collegiate Dutch Church is one of the oldest establishments of the kind in the city. Associated with this Church Association are the "North Church," in Fulton street; the new and elegant Church in Fifth avenue, corner of Twenty-ninth street; Ninth-street Church; and the Church on Lafayette Place.

THE DUTCH REFORMED CHURCH,

Situate on the east side of Washington Square, was erected in 1840, of rough granite. It is in the Gothic style, with a large centre window and two towers. Its interior is very finished and effective, especially the ornamental carved work of the organ, pulpit, etc.

THE FOURTH UNIVERSALIST CHURCH,

This is the Rev. Dr. Chapin's. Situated on the corner of Fifth avenue and Forty-fifth street. In the Gothic style with a frontage, including the towers, of 95 feet. The towers are 185 feet in height. The basement for Sunday-school, lecture-room, etc., extends under the entire church.

ST. PAUL'S METHODIST EPISCOPAL CHURCH,

On Fourth avenue, corner of Twenty-second street, is a magnificent edifice, built of marble, in the Romanesque style. The spire to this church (height 210 feet) is remarkable for its graceful proportions.

THE FIRST BAPTIST CHURCH,

Corner of Broome and Elizabeth streets, was erected in 1841. It is of the Gothic order, built of rough stone, with lintels, cornices and battlements of brown sandstone. It was constructed during the pastorate of the late Dr. Spencer H. Cone.

THE BRICK CHURCH

(Presbyterian) situate on the corner of Thirty-seventh street and Fifth avenue, is a spacious brick edifice, with a lofty spire.

GREENWOOD CEMETERY

Became a chartered institution in 1838. Its location was the result of a careful and extensive survey of the entire vicinity of New York. The enterprise, after four years of hard struggle, was at length placed upon a firm foundation, and the Cemetery was thrown open for interments in 1842. From that time its history has been one of uninterrupted progress. The original enclosure of one hundred and seventy-five acres has swelled, by successive additions on the west and south, to its present dimensions of 413 acres. Broad, substantial roads, underlaid with stones and bordered on the declivities with paved gutters, furnish, at all seasons, a hard and pleasant carriage path of many miles, and conduct the visitor to every part of the Cemetery. Commodious and inviting foot-paths wind round every hill, and explore each dell and shady nook. The water of Sylvan Lake is forced by steam power into an elevated reservoir, whence it is conveyed by pipes to different parts of the ground, to be used for irrigation and the supply of fountains.

The Cemetery is entered at its northwestern angle from the Fifth avenue, and also on the southern side from the old road known as Martense's Lane. The original entrance (and for many years the sole entrance) was a little south of what is now the northwestern corner of the grounds. This narrow passage-way, with its simple, rustic, yet picturesque lodge and bell-tower, was strictly in consonance with the limited purpose. The increasing number of visitors and of funerals, together with various annoyances which gathered, at length, around this only approach, led to the opening, in 1850, of what is now called the Western Entrance. During the twelve following years, visitors found admission to Greenwood almost wholly through this fine approach—the northern gate being appropriated to funerals.

The extension of the Fifth avenue, in 1862, upon a causeway of high grade, running directly by and across the Western Entrance, involved the necessity of a viaduct at that point. The stone archway built by the Trustees, over which the public travel passes, and through which visitors enter or leave the Cemetery, is a work that will compare, in solidity and beauty, with any similar structure in the country. This intrusion of the avenue makes a change of position necessary in regard to some of the buildings connected with this entrance, and they were accordingly removed to the western side of the viaduct. The gate-house here is a handsome wooden structure, with bell-tower and clock, rooms for the gate-keeper and family, and a room for visitors.

The Northern Entrance, commenced in 1861, was completed in 1863, and constitutes, henceforth, the principal entrance to the Cemetery. It is situated at that point of the ground which lies nearest to the vast population of New York and Brooklyn, and may be reached, at any hour of the day, by means of the horse-cars, which start in constant and frequent succession, from four ferries. Its outer gate, closed only at night, opens upon the Fifth avenue, directly opposite to the termination of Twenty-fifth street. An approach, graded with immense labor, and which, in a few years, will be beautifully shaded, leads, by a broad and gradually widening area, to the grand entrance. The great gateway, which faces the north, is an imposing and elaborate gothic edifice, solidly constructed of the best New Jersey sandstone. The passage-ways through the massive structure are appropriated—one to funerals, the other to visitors. A room for the latter to rest in, and fire-proof offices for the Cemetery business, occupy the lower part of the building. Upwards it terminates in three lofty pinnacles. The entire structure, built after designs by R. Upjohn & Son, is 132 feet, 6 inches long, and 40 feet deep. The central pinnacle is 146 feet high. There is a bell for the passing procession, and a clock to strike the hours. The deep, triangular recesses of the pediments above the two gate-ways are filled in, on both sides, with groups of sculpture formed of Nova Scotia sandstone. These four groups represent, in durable material and strong relief, viz.: The Saviour's Entombment; His Resurrection; the Resurrection of the Widow's son, and Raising of Lazarus. Still higher up, on the four shields which surmount the quatre-foils, are figures in relief of Faith, of Hope, of Memory, and of Love.

The entire surface of the Cemetery has been surveyed with trigonometrical precision, and has been divided into rectangular sections, where practicable, of three hundred square feet each. By reference to the field-book, in which these are all plotted, and where the occupied lots are duly entered, every foot of ground within the enclosure may be defined or identified with absolute certainty. As another result of this survey, a new and larger map has been constructed, and is ready for use. The visitor may now avail himself of a plain and perfectly reliable chart, on which he will find depicted not only numerous and various inequalities of these grounds, but all their avenues and paths clearly delineated and distinctly named.

It would be difficult to make anything like an accurate estimate of the vast amount which has been expended by individual proprietors on the many thousand lots already sold. Several hundred tombs have been constructed—and their vaults, whether placed in side hills or sunk in the ground, are generally of massive stone-work and durable masonry. The side-hill tombs are in most cases fronted by architectural facades, various in form and often beautiful. In addition to a great number of horizontal tablets, and small headstones, the Cemetery contains probably more than three thousand monuments, of marble, of sienite, or of sandstone. These vary greatly in magnitude and style, and range from forms quite simple and inexpensive, to others of great size and costly decoration. The number of interments made in the Cemetery is now about 170,000.

Since the time when, amid alternations of hope and discouragement, the foundations of this institution were laid, a great change has taken place in the public sentiment of our community. It is not now necessary to urge the manifold evils of intramural interment, or to present and portray the immense superiority of rural sepulture; for the former are no longer denied or doubted, and the latter has been practically demonstrated. The question may be looked upon as settled. Cities cease to endure within their limits the offensive and pestilential danger. The prejudices of early association, and even the ties of love and kindred, cannot longer reconcile the minds of any to the crowded church-yard vault.

Already, around our Greenwood cling the strong affections of many thousand hearts. Here lie the parent, the wife, the husband, the child, the lover, and the friend, once dearer to the surviving mourner than all else on earth. Hither often those survivors come to weep and meditate unseen. And here, by the mouldering relics of what was once so dear, do they hope, at last, to lie down themselves. Nor are these grounds destitute of that broader interest which attaches itself to the names and memories of those who have made themselves illustrious by deeds of greatness or lives of goodness. Here crumble the frail tenements in which learning and piety, patriotism and courage, once made their glorious home. If the brief experience of the past has accomplished so much, what expectations of the future may not safely be indulged? What tender associations, what kindling memories, what inspiring thoughts, will be awakened in the breasts of those who, at some coming and not distant day, shall explore this silent city of the dead!

While we allow that those who ride or drive through the principal avenues may see and may enjoy much, it is still true that the pedestrian alone becomes acquainted with Greenwood. He only finds the cross-roads, climbs the hills, dives into the dells, and wanders at will through scores of sequestered and leafy paths. Among the hundred and twenty-five thousand graves in this Cemetery there is many a monument, beautiful or queer; many an epitaph, appropriate or absurd, touching or laughable; many a memorial of true love and grief, as well as of harmless vanity and aping fashion, which the great majority of visitors never see and know nothing of. We would advise those who have the leisure to take one part at a time. Fix on a certain portion of the ground for the extent of a single ramble, and explore it thoroughly with your guide book and map.

Visitors are admitted to the grounds every day, (excepting Sundays, when lot owners only are privileged,) by procuring passes at the office of the Cemetery, No. 30 Broadway. Persons going to Greenwood can take either the Hamilton or Fulton Ferry boat to Brooklyn, thence by the horse cars, which run every few minutes, direct to the gate.

THE SUBURBS.

The suburbs of New York abound in picturesque retreats for the lover of rural beauty. Not only are abundant facilities rendered available to the pleasure tourist, in the multiplicity of modes of conveyance by land or by water, but the geographical position of the metropolis places within the circuit of a few miles almost every variety of beautiful scenery, as well as villages, towns, and localities of historic interest.

BROOKLYN.

Brooklyn, the city of churches, the third city in point of population, the principal suburb of New York, contains more than 500,000 inhabitants; and Brooklyn people believe, that ere many decades elapse, their city will be more populous than New York. Brooklyn is a city of dwelling-houses, occupied by people who do business in the city of New York. It is more readily accessible to the lower portion of the city than the upper part of the island is, and house rent is cheaper. It counts among its attractions a large number of churches, some few distinguished clergymen, and several *very sensational* ones. It has a very fine opera house, several theatres, and is just completing an art building which, for architectural beauty, will compare favorably with any building in the country. Prospect Park commands far more extensive and picturesque views than are to be had at Central Park. Greenwood Cemetery, previously described, is one of Brooklyn's chief attractions. Its Mercantile Library on Montague street, and the Long Island Historical Library, corner of Court and Joralemon streets, are thriving institutions, have a large number of members and readers, and offer all the attractions common to first-class libraries. Brooklyn now embraces what used to be known as Williamsburg.

THE NAVY YARD.

This is a place of interest to many travelers, and the Brooklyn yard is one of the best appointed in the country. It is located on Wallabout bay, about a mile from Fulton ferry. Cars from this ferry pass the yard, which is open to visitors daily from 10 A. M. to 3:30 P. M. On Tuesdays and Fridays visitors may be admitted on board the Receiving Ship.

STATEN ISLAND

Is a place of much attraction as a summer resort. Boats make the trip every hour, from Whitehall Dock near the Battery, to the east side of the Island, connecting with the Staten Island R. R. The North Shore Ferry is from Pier 19, E. R., to New Brighton, Port Richmond, etc. The scenery is exceedingly fine; and the drives to the Telegraph Station, Stapleton, Richmond, New Brighton, with their clusters of beautiful villas and country seats, are full of attraction.

HOBOKEN.

On the New Jersey shore is Hoboken, with its Elysian fields and pleasure grounds, the bold bluffs of Weehawken, the Sybil's cave, and the memorable spot of the duel between Colonel Burr and General Hamilton. The boats for Hoboken leave every few minutes, from the Barclay street and Christopher street ferries.

FLUSHING.

A pleasant trip to the entrance of Long Island Sound brings one to Flushing—a remarkably rural and picturesque town, with extensive botanic gardens, nurseries, and numerous elegant residences. It is a chosen suburban retreat of the New Yorkers. The Flushing boat leaves twice a day from the dock adjoining the Fulton ferry.

Bay Side, situated about four miles from Flushing, is a delightful place for a day's excursion; the scenery is beautiful, and the bay is famous for its clams—a roast of chowder served up in primitive style being one of the features of the place. This place can be reached by private conveyance only, but which can be obtained at Flushing at moderate charges.

GOVERNOR'S ISLAND

Is a military station of some importance, and may be reached by ferry from foot of Whitehall street, every hour from 8 A. M. to 6 P. M. The last boat leaves the Island after evening parade.

FORT HAMILTON,

An attractive place on the southwestern shore of Long Island, about five miles from the city.

CONEY ISLAND,

A short distance beyond Fort Hamilton, forms a part of Gravesend Township. It can be reached by boat from Pier No. 1, North River, or by cars from Brooklyn.

Time was when this sea-girt, barren sand-heap, was the only fashionable sea-bathing resort for New Yorkers, and when its beach was thronged with the beauty and the refinement of Manhattan Island and Brooklyn. But its nearness to the city, and the increasing facilities of reaching it, caused it to be speedily monopolized, with but few exceptions, by the rougher classes, and it was long ago abandoned by the "upper ten" for fresher waves and beaches new.

LONG BRANCH.

Long Branch, N. J., is thirty miles from New York, on the eastern shore, and has now become one of the most fashionable places of summer resort in the United States. During the summer season steamboats leave New York, from pier 28, N. R., for Sandy Hook, connecting there with New Jersey Southern Railway for Long Branch.

For those who enjoy sea-bathing, Long Branch offers particular inducements.

ROCKAWAY BEACH.

Visitors to Rockaway Beach proceed from New York to Brooklyn, thence by South Side Railway *via* Jamaica. The beach affords excellent bathing, and has become quite a fashionable watering-place.

JAMAICA,

Which is easy of access by the L. I. Railroad, South Ferry, is an interesting old rural town, and is the highway of communication to Hempstead, Greenpoint, Rockaway and Montauk.

THROG'S POINT

Is another pleasing excursion, sixteen miles from the city. It is the termination, at Long Island Sound, of Throg's or rather Throgmorton's Neck. From this headland, which divides the East River from the Sound, a very splendid view is obtained. Fort Schuyler on the point, and Pelham Bridge, may be embraced in this excursion.

ASTORIA.

An eighth excursion may take for its terminus the thriving village of Astoria, six miles to the north-east of New York. The academy, botanic gardens, etc., are worthy of notice; but its most interesting feature is the singular whirlpool in its neighborhood, denominated "*Helle Gat*," by the Dutch. The Government are now engaged at Willett's Point in one of the most gigantic engineering difficulties of modern times, viz: the entire removal of the rocks which form the whirlpool, and that have heretofore greatly impeded the navigation of the

Sound for large vessels. This great work will be completed, it is said, by the 4th of July, 1876, when the immense charges of giant powder deposited in the tunnels and galleries under the river will be exploded, and thus at once relieve the river of a dangerous obstruction and sound a fitting salute to our centennial holiday.

MONTAUK,

On the extremity of Long Island, and almost surrounded by water, affords a magnificent view of the broad Atlantic, which here skirts the horizon in almost every direction. One of the most interesting features of the neighborhood is a remnant of the pure Indian still living on the eastern extremity of the coast. They mostly subsist by fishing, their dress and manners are rude and picturesque and they still retain, in a small measure, the dialect of their red forefathers.

CROTON DAM.

A visit to the great Croton Aqueduct is one of the most interesting expeditions, as well as the easiest, that could be devised. The village of Croton is about 35 miles from the city, which is reached best by the Hudson River Railroad. The famous dam pertaining to the works is well worthy of a visit. The lake, measuring five miles, covers an area of 400 acres; it is formed by a dam 250 feet long, and 38 feet wide at the base, allowing a discharge of 60 million gallons of water daily.

CREEDMOOR,

Twelve miles from Hunter's Point, on the line of the Central Railroad. These are the grounds of the National Rifle Association, and are well worthy a visit. Although this Association is as yet in its infancy, having been established but two seasons, it has already produced marksmen that have been able to successfully compete with the chosen shots of England. During the season the grounds are open every day from sunrise to sunset; only members, however, are permitted to practice at the ranges, others are admitted on payment of a small fee; *ladies free.*

FORTS AND FORTIFICATIONS.

The national defences of New York comprise the following: The strong fortifications of the Narrows. On the one side Fort Tompkins and Fort Richmond at the lower verge of the Staten Island shore. These fortifications are quite new, are constructed of gray stone, mounted with guns of large calibre, and are among the most imposing objects that first greet the vision of passenger from the water waste. The water-battery is the most fort-like in appearance, but, in the event of a fleet of iron-clads undertaking to force an entrance, would probably prove more vulnerable than the batteries on the heights, from which a continuous volley of plunging shot could be directed with as much effect as from Gibralter or any stronghold in the world.

Opposite, on the Long Island shore, is the formidable Fort Hamilton, which numbers in its armament several of the celebrated Rodman guns, whose iron spherical shot of one thousand pounds would prove disagreeable to the sides of almost any iron ship-of-war that floats; and also the old, round, red Fort Lafayette, isolated in the waves, and likely to prove more famous as a rebel prison than as an impregnable fortress in these days of improved warfare.

To protect the inner harbor, there are Fort Columbus and Castle William on Governor's Island, and the works on Bedloe's and Ellis Islands.

Castle William, measuring 600 feet in circumference, and 60 feet high, is a circular stone battery connecting with Fort Columbus on the same Island. Here are barracks and a corps of U. S. troops.

Governor's Island, formerly known as Nut Island, from its formerly being covered with nut trees, was, in colonial times, used by the English Governors as a pleasure ground. The several fortifications here may be easily seen by taking a boat from Castle Garden, foot of the Battery.

The East River or Sound defences consist of Fort Schuyler on Throg's Neck, a large, three-tier gun fortification, built of gray granite. Opposite, on the Long Island shore, the government are erecting new works of both granite and earth. These, when completed, it is expected will amply protect the city from any hostile fleet approaching from the direction of Long Island Sound.

DIRECTORY TO ADVERTISEMENTS.

BATHS (Russian).

		Page.
"IMPERIAL"	7 West 24th Street	16

BATHS (Turkish).

GIBSON	Broadway and 13th Street	40

BILLIARD TABLE MANUFACTURER.

COLLENDER	738 Broadway	Opposite inside back cover.

BOOTS AND SHOES.

ALEXANDER	357 Sixth Avenue	18
BIXBY	8 Astor Place	78
COHN	281 Grand Street	110
CONNER	311 Sixth Avenue	98
SLATER	{ 878 Broadway / 1143 Broadway }	10
THIERRY	846 Broadway	78
TILSON & CHARDE	635 Sixth Avenue	52

CAMEO PORTRAITS.

BONET	599 Broadway	94

CANDY AND SUGAR PLUMS.

RIDLEY	{ 1149 Broadway / Chambers and Hudson Street }	100

CARRIAGE MANUFACTORY.

HAM	10 to 20 East 4th Street	90

CHAIR SEATS.

"EUREKA"	110 Bowery	36

CHINA AND GLASSWARE.

BRUNDIGE	{ 919 Broadway / 654 Sixth Avenue }	56
SHAW	25 Duane Street	58

COMMISSIONAIRE COMPANY.

"THE NEW YORK"	Fourth Ave. and 14th Street	72

CONSERVATORY OF MUSIC.

"THE GRAND"	Fifth Avenue	116

CORSETS.

DE WAIBEL	27 East 18th Street	114

CIGARS.

LEVY	848 Broadway	110

INDEX TO ADVERTISEMENTS.

DENTISTRY.
		Page.
ALLEN	314 Fifth Avenue	46
COLTON	19 Cooper Institute	92
MEADER	262 Sixth Avenue	98

DRESSMAKING.
DONAVAN	8 East 18th Street	88
GEDNEY	19 West 30th Street	114
LORD & TAYLOR	Broadway and 20th Street	50
MOSCHCOWITZ & RUSSELL	21 University Place	114

DRESS AND UPHOLSTERY TRIMMINGS.
CROSLEY	900 Broadway	88

DRY GOODS.
BLOOM	338 & 340 Bowery	40
DANIELL	759 Broadway	62
LE BOUTILLIER	48 East 14th Street	102
MACY	14th Street and Sixth Avenue	28
MEARES	Sixth Avenue and 19th Street	104

DUMB WAITERS.
MURTAUGH	1370 Broadway	80

DYERS.
BARRETTS, PALMER & HEAL	484 Broadway	86
"THE NEW YORK"	98 Duane Street	84
"THE STATEN ISLAND"	5 & 7 John Street	84

EMBROIDERIES AND WORSTEDS.
KORFF	230 Fifth Avenue	12
KUHN	941 Broadway	20

FASHIONS.
SMITH	914 Broadway	60

FERROTYPES, NON-REVERSED.
ESTABROOKE	31 Union Square	68

FRENCH FANCY GOODS.
DEVIN	1192 Broadway	18

FURS.
MAHLER	649 Broadway	12
SHAYNE	Broadway and 10th Street	112

GENTS' FURNISHING GOODS.
FLING	178 Fifth Ave	16

GROCERIES, WINES AND CIGARS.
JACKSON	{ 182 Fifth Ave. { 18 & 20 College Place }	Inside back cover.

HAIR DYE.
EGYPTIAN HAIR COLORING		76

HAND-MADE WORSTEDS.
LOVE	{ 313 Sixth Ave. } { 1197 Broadway }	14

HATTER.
DUNLAP	{ 174 Fifth Ave.. } { 559 Broadway.. }	34

HATS—Fur, Wool and Straw.

		Page.
STICH & BROMBERG	39 Mercer Street	96

HOUSE FURNISHING HARDWARE.

NEWMAN & CAPRON	1172 Broadway	30
JONES	920 Broadway	90

HOUSEKEEPING GOODS.

EDGAR	389 Sixth Ave	52

HUMAN HAIR.

SHAW	361 Bowery / 345 Sixth Ave.	42

INDUSTRIAL EXHIBITION.

MORGENTHAU, BRUNO & CO.	23 Park Row	36

IVORY GOODS.

GROTE	114 East 14th Street	102

KNITTING MACHINE.

SCHIFF & HETZEL	306 Grand Street	175

LACES AND EMBROIDERIES.

MILLER & GRANT	879 Broadway	106

LIFE INSURANCE.

"KNICKERBOCKER"	239 Broadway	18

MAGNETIC SALVE.

STEINFELD	306 Grand Street	175

MEAT EXTRACT.

DANNHEIM	100 Chambers Street	Inside front cover.

MILLINER.

BROWN	1261 Broadway	114

MUSICAL BOXES.

PAILLARD	680 Broadway	26

OPTICIANS.

PIKE	518 Broadway	64
QUEEN	601 Broadway	58
SEMMONS	687 Broadway	74
WALDSTEIN	545 Broadway	32

PARLOR ORGANS.

WATERS	481 Broadway	54, 59

PERFUMERY AND TOILET GOODS.

ATWOOD	846 Broadway	106

PHOTOGRAPHERS.

BROWNELL & JEWELL	889 Broadway	82
JOHNSON	777 Broadway	70
KURTZ	23d Street, opp. Madison Square	82

REFRIGERATORS.

"THE ZERO"	224 & 226 West 23d Street	100

SALLE D'ARMES.

MONSTERY	619 Sixth Avenue	

INDEX TO ADVERTISEMENTS.

SHADES AND ROLLERS (PATENT).
Page.
EATON..................14 Park Place............................. 76

SHIRTS.
SMITH................683 Broadway............................. 32

SILVER PLATED WARE.
LANDER................18 John Street......................... 8

SILVERSMITHS.
GORHAM MANUFACTURING CO....4 Bond Street................. 6

SILVER WARE.
RICE..................527 Broadway.................Opposite title.

SOAP.
"ZIRCON"..............1 Barclay Street....................... 108

STATIONERS AND PRINTERS.
FRANCIS & LOUTREL......45 Maiden Lane...................... 20
McDONALD, DILLONT & CO....1 Park Place................... 22

STORAGE.
BATTERSON.............595 & 597 Sixth Avenue............... 44

TAILOR.
WILLMONT..............663 Broadway.......................... 14

TOILETTE PREPARATIONS.
GOURNE................101 West 22d Street................... 74

TOYS AND FANCY GOODS.
HINRICHS..............29, 31 & 33 Park Place................ 66

TRUNKS.
CHERRY................592 Sixth Avenue..................... 96
GILLMORE..............26 Fourth Avenue..................... 26

TRUSSES AND SUPPORTERS.
ELASTIC TRUSS CO......683 Broadway......................... 41
POMEROY...............744 Broadway......................... 108

VIENNA LEATHER GOODS.
CULBERT...............24 Maiden Lane....................... 8

WATCHES AND JEWELRY.
BYNNER................527 Broadway..............Opposite title.
JOHNSTON..............150 Bowery........Opposite inside front cover.
PHELPS................677 Sixth Avenue..................... 94
TIFFANY...............Union Square........................... 24

WATCH IMPORTER.
BARTENS...............3 John Street........................ 92

WEATHER STRIPS.
BROWNE'S..............812 Broadway......................... 80

BUY THE FRANZ & POPE AUTOMATIC KNITTING MACHINE, AND YOU WILL HAVE THE VERY BEST

Can be recommended for family as well as manufacturing purposes on account of its simplicity, durability and cheapness. With the aid of the instruction book, the operation of this Knitter can be learned by a child of 6 years.

This machine knits a sock, with heel and toe complete, in five minutes; and persons who are incapacitated for hard work can earn from two to four dollars per day, and ladies who have taste for fancy work can get up from a Watch Guard to a Sleigh Robe, on this Knitter, in a wonderfully short time.

SCHIFF & HETZEL,
GENERAL AGENTS
(Opposite Ridley's),

306 Grand Street (up stairs). NEW YORK.

DR. R. STEINFELD'S
MAGNETIC SALVE AND DROPS,
FOR SALE AT M. SCHIFF'S.

306 Grand Street (up stairs). - - NEW YORK.

Is recommended by thousands of ladies and gentlemen, who have used this Salve with success

AGENTS WANTED EVERYWHERE.
PLEASE SEND FOR CIRCULAR.

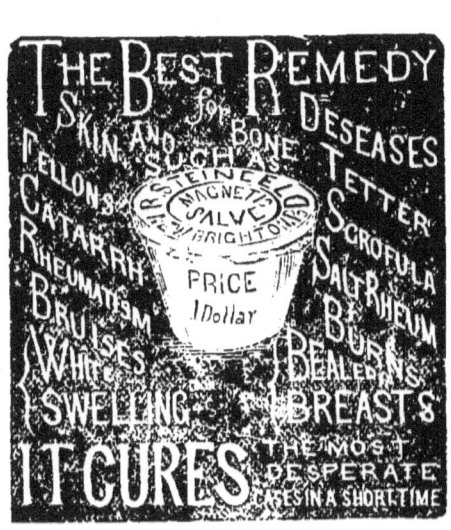

THE BEST REMEDY for DESEASES SKIN AND BONE SUCH AS TETTER FELLONS CATARRH SCROFULA RHEUMATISM SALT RHEUM BRUISES BURNS WHITE DEALERS SWELLING BREASTS IT CURES THE MOST DESPERATE CASES IN A SHORT TIME

STEINFELD MAGNETIC SALVE NEW BRIGHTON PRICE 1 Dollar

Dr. Steinfeld's Magnetic Drops are purely vegetable, and are among the best remedies for Dyspepsia or Indigestion, for strengthening the nervous system and purifying the blood.

STANDARD AMERICAN BILLIARD TABLES.

NEW DESIGN, PATENTED JUNE 6, 1871, AND DEC. 23, 1873.

[Entered according to Act of Congress, by H. W. Collender, in Office of Librarian of Congress, Washington, 1871.]

The above design is made in Walnut, Rosewood, Hungarian Ash, or other woods. The STANDARD AMERICAN TABLES are furnished with the unrivalled

PHELAN & COLLENDER COMBINATION CUSHION,

Demanded by all intelligent amateur players, and used by experts in all their important test games. The characteristics which have given these tables a world-wide reputation are

First Class Workmanship, Uniformity of Construction and Durability.

Everything appertaining to Billiards kept constantly on hand. Send for illustrated circular and price-list. Address, Box 1847, New York Post Office.

H. W. COLLENDER,

Successor to PHELAN & COLLENDER.

738 BROADWAY.

SPECIAL NOTICE.—In consequence of the death of Mr. Phelan, the firm of PHELAN & COLLENDER is dissolved. The undersigned, the surviving partner, begs to inform the customers of the house, and the public generally, that having purchased the entire stock—machinery, copy-rights, trade-marks and letters patent of the late firm, he continues the business in the same extensive manufactory, *Thirty-sixth Street, Thirty-seventh Street and Tenth Avenue,* and at the well known wareroom, *No. 738 Broadway,* at either of which places he will be happy to meet customers for the transaction of new business, or to settle up the affairs of the old firm.

Respectfully,

H. W. COLLENDER.

www.ingramcontent.com/pod-product-compliance
Lightning Source LLC
Chambersburg PA
CBHW032157160426
43197CB00008B/951